Keeping It Real

Teens Write About Peer Pressure

By Youth Communication

Edited by Al Desetta

True Stories by Teens

D1417700

Keeping It Real

EXECUTIVE EDITORS
Keith Hefner and Laura Longhine

CONTRIBUTING EDITORS
Andrea Estepa, Hope Vanderberg, Rachel Blustain, Al Desetta, Clarence Haynes, Katia Hetter, Philip Kay, Sasha Chavkin, and Tamar Rothenberg

LAYOUT & DESIGN
Efrain Reyes, Jr. and Jeff Faerber

COVER ART
Stephanie Wilson

For reprint information, please contact Youth Communication.

ISBN 978-1-933939-76-6

Second, Expanded Edition

Printed in the United States of America

Youth Communication ®
New York, New York
www.youthcomm.org

Dedication

૭૦   ୦੩

We dedicate this first book in a series of more than
50 books by teens at Youth Communication to
Julie Jensen
who believes deeply
that young people's voices should be heard.
Thanks to her vision and support,
more young people will benefit from these stories
than we ever imagined.

Table of Contents

Contents

Contents

Introduction

The author of "My Secret Love," one of 18 true stories in *Keeping It Real*, was born and raised in a rough neighborhood where he learned "to walk and talk tough." Because of the way he looks and dresses, his peers expect him to listen to hip-hop music 24/7, and in fact he does like rap.

But there's another side to the writer that he hides from his friends. He loves musicals—*The Sound of Music, The King and I, Carousel, West Side Story*. If his peers find out, he'll be ridiculed. Enjoying a different kind of music from everyone else, he writes, is more taboo than having a drug problem: "I'm afraid to come out of my creative closet because I want to avoid being mocked."

All the writers in this book confront a similar dilemma—they face a moment where they have to decide whether to go along with what their friends want them to do, or to be their own person, even if that means being alone or having to find new friends.

One summer, Jamel Salter's friends decide to try smoking marijuana for the first time.

"I sat at the end of the line," Jamel writes, "hoping that they would finish the blunt before it got to me or that someone else would turn it down so that I wouldn't be the only one who refused. Neither happened, and I found myself being handed the blunt."

At that moment, Jamel has to choose: "It was a choice between smoking and keeping their friendship or not smoking and keeping my health. I came to my senses and just passed it on." The decision is not without a price—Jamel sticks to his principles, but loses his friends. Although the price is high, Jamel is not sorry about the choice he made.

Keeping It Real shows teens dealing with peer pressure in a wide range of situations. Lenny Jones, who is black, regrets ending a relationship with his girlfriend, who is white, because of negative reactions to interracial dating. Fan Yi Mok faces pressure to cheat on tests at her elite high school. The female author of "The Trouble with Being a Virgin" pretends she is not a virgin so she can relate better to her sexually active female friends, while Damon Washington, unlike most of his male peers, is proud that he's never had sex and refuses to follow the crowd.

These writers don't hide the fact that going against the grain can be lonely. As Charlene George writes in "Can't Afford to Follow":

"I resolved to stop smoking, drinking, and hanging out with my old friends. After school I'd go home and watch TV during my free time. I was being a good person, but I got really bored and lonely. I felt like I was walking through a maze trying to find some new friends."

It takes a while, but Charlene, like other writers in this book, finds new friends who don't pressure her to do things she doesn't want to do.

The teens also remind us that peer pressure can be a positive force.

"If an opportunity comes along, like a scholarship or a great job," writes Desiree Bailey of her group of friends, "we encourage each other to take it." Jill Feigelman's friends urge her to join the high school's dance company, and she's glad they did.

"I was happy my friends had kept bugging me to join because I needed their encouragement," she writes. "Their positive peer pressure pushed me to do something I really loved."

Most of all, these writers show us how they mature and grow when they follow their own paths. The author of "Thinking for Myself" faces so much pressure to conform from friends, advertising, and mainstream culture that she leaves her home in New York for a year to live in an alternative community in Colorado.

"I didn't have a cell phone, TV, or radio. I didn't go to any malls or use the Internet," she writes. "Slowly, I became a different person."

When she returns to New York to finish high school, she realizes she doesn't have to run from peer pressure, but can simply walk away and make other choices.

These courageous stories show how real teens have managed two often conflicting desires: to be accepted, and to be true to themselves.

In the following story, names have been changed: *Why I Speak My Mind, My So-Called Friends, Why Do So Many Teens Cheat?, The Pastor's Daughter, The Trouble with Being a Virgin,* and *Thinking for Myself.*

Santiago Tau

My Secret Love

By Anonymous

I was born and raised in a rough neighborhood, where I learned to walk and talk tough. I know who to watch out for on the street, like dudes who carry liquor bottles and wear too much red. (There are a lot of gang members around my way.)

The way I dress reflects my neighborhood, so most people expect my taste in music to follow the same pattern. Mean streets + the latest jeans + the latest hairstyle + Timberlands = hard-core rap 24/7.

That's partially true, because hip-hop is a major part of my life. But there's also a hidden part of me. It's not something I like to talk about. If I did, people would laugh long and loud. It's not easy for me to admit this, but. . .

I love musicals.

Yep. *The Sound of Music, The King and I, Carousel, West Side*

Story. . . you name it, I've seen and enjoyed it.

I like the emotions given off by musicals, the way the story and the songs blend together to make a single presentation filled with dancing and catchy show tunes. I like watching Mary Poppins fly around with an umbrella, singing about medicine going down nicely if you take sugar with it.

But you're not listening. You're too busy laughing at me. The way I began this story, you probably thought I had a drug problem. If I did, I would have gladly put my name on this article. No one would laugh at me if I was addicted to cocaine.

Musicals and I go way back. *The Sound of Music* was the first one I saw, back in 6th grade. My teacher rolled the TV into the room, switched the lights off, and let the show begin. I sighed and braced myself for what I thought would be the whackest class of my 11 years.

But then, when the characters started singing, it suddenly became interesting to me. Characters would be talking about something, then they would just jump into song. As I watched the film, I realized I was being introduced to a revolutionary concept—a full-length movie that conveyed emotions through music and singing.

In one of the most memorable scenes, the main character, Maria (played by Julie Andrews), comforts the kids she is taking care of. The children are scared of a raging storm, so she begins to sing about her "favorite things" to take their minds off their fear.

A few weeks after the viewing, the entire school had to do renditions of various musical numbers on stage in the auditorium. My class had to sing "Sixteen Going on Seventeen" from *The Sound of Music*. One part was sung by the girls and the other part by the fellas. We did well, and my self-confidence never faltered during the performance.

But after my performance in 6th grade, I lost interest. My attention span was really short when it came to new things. Musicals were the last thing on my mind until my senior year of high school.

My music teacher rekindled my interest. He showed flicks like *Carousel* and *West Side Story* to our class every week as examples of different kinds of music. The other kids didn't appreciate it at all, but every day I secretly hoped he'd continue showing them.

My music teacher was gay and white, so admitting that he liked musicals didn't hurt his reputation at all. I, on the other hand, wouldn't be able to take the "Oh yeah, he's gay too" stares I knew I would get if people knew my secret.

But one day, I took a chance and admitted to some friends at work that I had watched a few musicals.

"Come on, sing a show tune you know," someone said.

"Yeah, don't be shy."

"Why not?" I said after a moment's hesitation.

I attempted to repeat my stellar 6th grade performance in response to the earnest requests of my co-workers. So I started singing that still familiar song in a mock soprano voice.

"I am 16, going on 17, I know that I'm naïve…fellows I meet may tell me I'm sweet, and willingly I beleeeeive…"

(OK, so for some strange reason, I only remembered the girl's part.)

There's a black kid I know who listens to a rock band all the time. But he doesn't tell anyone because he fears being ridiculed by his peers.

Instead of applause for my attempt to bestow culture upon them, what followed was 10 minutes of uncontrollable laughter. And mocking.

Ingrates.

But really, what's so bad about liking musicals? The music is catchy and you have visuals. They're similar to the modern music video, but they differ because videos focus mainly on money, drugs, sex, or violence in its rawest form. A lot of these topics are watered down in most musicals because they were made in the beginning and middle of the century, when things were less explicit.

But today's teens can still relate to many of the messages that musicals convey. For instance, in *West Side Story*, Officer Krupke pisses off the Jets gang royally. They want to go out and release their anger violently, which would've sent them straight to the slammer.

Instead, they perform a dance and song, "Cool," which helps them control themselves and avoid getting arrested. It was similar to Michael Jackson's "Beat It" video in terms of attitude and how they would lash out unexpectedly with a "Pow!" or "Bam!"

Even though musicals and music videos have many similarities, kids my age who come from the block would probably never allow themselves to appreciate show tunes unless they're being sampled by rappers. The dudes in my neighborhood and high school are all about rap and r&b. They'd rather listen to rhymes in Japanese than take in alternative styles.

There's a black kid I know who listens to a rock band all the time. But he doesn't tell anyone because he fears being ridiculed by his peers. He expresses his love for alternative music only to his closest friends. Like him, I'm afraid to come out of my creative closet because I want to avoid being mocked.

But it's still unfair. Just because I'm a rough dude who happens to like watching films where people abruptly break into song and dance shouldn't automatically draw people to the conclusion that I'm a freak.

I don't want to be the butt of jokes or to be looked at as pitiful. I don't want people to say, "My life is messed up, but I'm better than the cat who likes musicals."

I just don't get it. Why can't I sing songs from The King and I in peace?

The writer was 17 when he wrote this story.
He later attended college.

Victor Aviles

Losing My Friends to Weed

By Jamel A. Salter

I had a lot of friends who I grew up with, and growing up together made us very close—until my friends got too close to weed.

Before that happened, we were always together. We'd go to movies, parties, the park, and if we didn't have anywhere to go, we'd stay at one of our houses and play video games.

Even though we were close friends, we still had our little arguments. But when we argued, Dave would get in the middle and try to stop it. He was like the official peacemaker of the group.

Dave had the best sense of humor out of all of us. He was always telling jokes. That was one of the best things about hanging with them—you always got a good laugh.

But one day, when my friends were about 14, they made plans to put money in to buy some weed. I didn't want to put any money in because I didn't want to have anything to do with weed. I thought if I didn't put any money in they would say I couldn't smoke and I would pretend I was disappointed. But they got enough money to go through with it and said I could smoke anyway.

Someone had to ride his bike 35 blocks to go get it. (The things people do for drugs!) We were at the park when they started smoking it. One person lit the blunt, took a puff, and passed it around. I was in total shock because I had read and seen about drugs on television and here it was right in front of me.

As it was going around I was thinking to myself, "What should I do. Should I say yes or no?" I looked at how my friends were reacting after they smoked it. Since it was their first time, everyone coughed hard after they took a puff.

I sat at the end of the line, hoping that they would finish the blunt before it got to me or that someone else would turn it down so that I wouldn't be the only one who refused. Neither happened, and I found myself being handed the blunt.

"Chill yo, I don't want any."

"Take a puff son, it's mad nice."

"If you don't smoke, you're a herb."

"You can't be a mama's boy the rest of your life."

I got so tempted that I actually took it in my hand. But I knew that it was a choice between smoking and keeping their friendship or not smoking and keeping my health. I came to my senses and just passed it on.

"You really are a herb."

"You can't hang, mama's boy."

When they finished smoking, they started acting like fools. They were hitting each other and cracking stupid jokes. Seeing the way they acted made me glad that I didn't smoke. The next day everyone was talking about how bad they felt in the morning. You would think that would make them come to their senses and stop, but they just started making plans to get more.

My friends have been smoking for a year now and it has changed them. They always look like zombies. Their eyes are always red and halfway closed. They have bad tempers and they are always ready to fight. Especially Dave. Now he has the baddest temper of them all.

A few weeks ago we were at the park playing basketball. Dave had the ball and when I tried to steal it from him, I slapped his hand by accident. He got highly upset and started yelling at me.

"Why the hell are you fouling me?"

"It was an accident, and I don't know what you're getting mad about anyway," I told him. "It's all a part of the game. If you can't deal with it, don't play."

Dave tried to punch me but missed, then the others held him back and calmed him down. This surprised me because Dave was always the peacemaker before he began to smoke pot.

I sat at the end of the line, hoping that they would finish the blunt before it got to me.

My friends and I always used to play against other blocks in basketball, and I always started. I didn't hear about a game for a while but I didn't worry, because I figured my friends would tell me when they were playing. Then one day I called Dave to see what he was doing and his mother picked up.

"Hello, this is Jamel. Is Dave there?"

"No, he isn't, Jamel. He went to the park about a half hour ago."

When I got to the park I saw them just finishing playing the other team. I got upset because I always started and now, because I don't smoke weed, they didn't even bother to call me. (By the way, they lost.)

Not being close to my friends like I used to be makes me think to myself, "Maybe I should smoke it just one time. What's the worst thing that could happen to me?" Then I remember the way that they were acting the other day in the park and I just forget about it.

You might be wondering why I don't stop trying to stay close to them and make new friends, but it isn't so easy to lose friends you've grown up with. I keep trying to talk them out of smoking, because I don't want that stuff to make them sick. But they just laugh as if I'm stupid and tell me to mind my own business.

It's hard to believe that the difference between friends or no friends comes from one little blunt.

I wish our friendship could go back to the way it was before, but I don't think there's any chance of that happening while they keep smoking. I used to think that they were true friends, but now I know that it was just a game.

If not smoking is the reason why I've lost my friends, then I've been cheated. It's hard to believe that the difference between friends or no friends comes from one little blunt.

Jamel was 16 when he wrote this story.

Antoine B. Platel

Why Do So Many Teens Cheat?

By Fan Yi Mok

During my first chemistry test at my new high school, I was surprised to find the guy sitting next to me glancing over at my paper. It took me a moment to realize what he was doing.

"No, he's not cheating," I thought. "He's so smart."

But on the second test there was no denying it. He was clearly looking at my paper.

He wasn't the only cheater. After the first test, a girl in my class discussed it with me in the gym locker room.

"Did you hear papers rustling during the test?" Anne asked me.

"No."

"Oh, thank goodness! I had my notebook open under my desk and I was so nervous when the teacher was walking around the room," she said.

Naively, I asked why she did it. Anne looked at me curiously and wrinkled her brow as she just shrugged it off. Cheating — a typical activity that teen-agers engage in. No need to dwell on it.

I, on the other hand, was shocked and appalled. I couldn't believe that a person would cheat on one of the first tests of the year. Talk about starting off on the wrong foot. What offended me most, though, was Anne's indifference.

I soon learned that Anne's view on cheating was not unique. The student union vice president at my high school was forced to resign last fall after she was caught cheating on a chemistry test.

For many students, what was controversial was that she had to resign, not that she cheated. While riding the school's escalator, I overheard a student saying he thought the decision was unjust. "I bet that if you ask anyone in this school, they'll tell you that they've cheated before," he said.

His thinking seems to be that if the majority does something, no matter how dishonest it is, it should be accepted.

Others feel the pressure to cheat because, to them, grades are indicators of success, accomplishment, and character.

And it's not only at my school. After talking to students from several New York City high schools, I discovered that cheating is an accepted part of our academic life.

One senior told me, "Cheating is bad, but when it comes down to either cheating or going to summer school, I'd rather cheat."

All the students I talked to felt like the guy on the escalator — cheating's acceptable because almost everybody does it.

"Everyone cheats every now and then," said one sophomore.

"It's not something to be proud of, but like everyone cheats," said another sophomore.

Why do so many teenagers cheat? For starters, we're under a

lot of pressure to perform. From the time we're young, many of us are bombarded with the idea that doing well in school is the surest way to guarantee a successful future.

According to a sophomore I spoke with, many students fear that "their parents, friends, or teachers will be disappointed" if their grades don't measure up. Many also worry about the effect their grades will have on their college acceptance or ability to get scholarships.

Others are simply worried about passing the class and graduating on time. As a friend of mine put it, "Almost all the people I know and have known through school didn't care about 'remaining on top.' They just wanted to pass and get out of school."

And others feel the pressure to cheat because, to them, grades are indicators of success, accomplishment, and character. They think that by getting high grades, students show the world they can measure up to an ideal.

One sophomore told me he sometimes cheats because he doesn't want "to be looked upon as a below-average or unintelligent individual" by doing poorly on a test.

Competition is another reason why some students cheat. For overachievers, every digit and grade counts.

In schools like the one I go to, where grades in the 90s are common, many may feel the need to cheat to keep themselves one step ahead. As the guy who cheated in chemistry explained, "In a competitive academic environment, one needs to take every advantage they can get."

When I transferred to my current high school, I'd expected competitiveness, but I was caught off guard by the attitude toward grades. Earlier this year when transcripts were handed out, I saw my peers scramble to find out each other's averages, down to the decimals.

People I barely knew casually asked me what my transcript average was, oblivious to a little something called manners. The obsession over grades even made people resentful towards the highest scorer on a test. But it was the amount of cheating that bothered me the most.

I thought it was strange that cheating seemed even more rampant at my new high school, where admission involved sitting through a two-and-a-half-hour written test. I assumed that since my school's population was filled with skilled test-takers, they would have less of a need to cheat.

But after hearing stories from other schools, I've come to believe that cheating goes on everywhere. It probably just seems worse at my school—because everyone is so grade-obsessed, they talk about it all the time.

My friend Sarah, a good student with a strong work ethic, is not someone I would have expected to cheat. But one day, joining me at the usual table during lunch period, she announced: "I just had a quiz in Spanish." Then she added, with a laugh, "I cheated through that whole thing."

I too am starting to feel the pressure to take the cheater's way out.

Her carefree attitude irked me, so I asked her why she did it.

"It's Spanish," was her explanation.

Hold on there. What makes it more acceptable to cheat on a Spanish test than, let's say, a math test? Sarah explained that sometimes people don't prioritize studying for something like a small Spanish quiz when there are more important things, "such as family issues or a larger term paper or exam."

Many students who don't cheat all the time feel that it is "OK" to cheat in certain situations, although how they determine that is complex.

Some people believe that when a test really counts, students won't cheat because the consequences of getting caught are too high. One friend doesn't cheat on major exams like the SAT or "major subject tests" because of this.

Students might also cheat in a class that isn't being taught well, out of spite, or in a class that they view as too easy, uninteresting, or unimportant to bother studying for. Others cheat on the subject that is hardest for them.

Even though I still think cheating is wrong, I too am starting to feel the pressure to take the cheater's way out. The demands of high school and being a teenager are so overwhelming at times that I don't get to study for a science or history quiz. Cheating becomes the more appealing option when the other choice is to fail.

Fan Yi was 16 when she wrote this story. She attended Hunter College after graduating from high school.

Matty DeLuna

Can't Afford to Follow

By Charlene George

I heard the same things from my new friends at middle school nearly every day. "Yo, Charlene, let's not go to school today. Let's go smoke and get some alcohol. Let's maybe go to the movies, museum, or the zoo, but let's not go to school today."

They seemed really nice, and when they spoke about all the fun places they went during school, I decided to join them. I wanted to hang out with them and be the type of friend they said was cool.

One day we went to the movie theater and saw five movies— but we only paid for one. It was so great to see action, funny, and scary movies that had just come out, all in one day.

Then my friends told me to steal $20 from my foster mom so we could go to the movies again. They also wanted me to buy some things for them. I didn't want to let them down, so I said

OK. But I couldn't bring myself to steal from my mom. Instead, I brought $20 I'd saved up and pretended that I'd stolen it from her.

I 'd lived with my foster mom since I was 7 years old. I felt she really wanted the best for me. I wondered why my friends never wanted to talk about their own families, and why none of them could say even one good thing about their parents.

But I kept on doing things with my friends to show that I was one of them. About three weeks after I started cutting school with them, we went to the mall. We didn't have any money, so we were just window-shopping and looking around in a store called Rainbow.

Then, to my surprise, my mother's good friend Kim popped out of the back. It turned out that she worked there. She asked me what I was doing there during school hours.

Before I could answer, the man who worked at the counter started yelling at my friends. It wasn't a pretty sight the way he was grabbing them, like his nails were digging into their skin. Their bodies were leaning to the side and they were screaming, "Help, he's hurting me!"

My friends told me to steal $20 from my mom so we could go to the movies.

When the boss went over to the counter to see what was going on, I was shocked. My friends had been stealing small items like candy, earrings, and fake rings that would turn your fingers green in a second. He called the police and my friends looked afraid, like they were wondering where their lives were headed now.

When the police came, they needed my friends' family information so their parents could come get them. Most of them had their parents come to pick them up. But when the police asked the two ringleaders of our group about their families, they looked shocked.

They said they didn't have any information to give the police.

For the first time, I suspected that they didn't have anyone taking care of them to come pick them up.

As they left the store, it hit me that maybe they cut school and stole things because they had no one taking care of them and teaching them how to act. But I did, so why was I acting this way? I imagined being locked up away from my mother, just because I wanted to be a follower. I thought to myself that my future couldn't be a jail cell. It had to be a home and family.

I was lucky to have my foster mother and I didn't want to lose her. I asked myself, "Am I going to let this peer pressure keep getting to me?" Doing what they asked me to do was only getting me in trouble.

Luckily, while my friends were stealing, I'd been standing next to Kim. After the police left, Kim made sure that I went home right away. She said she knew that I wasn't the type to steal. She said, "I'm not going to tell your mom," and that made me feel really happy.

Then she said, "You have to tell her all by yourself. Letting your mom know would show her what you did wrong, but it would also show that you're growing up."

I was upset. I'd hoped that Kim would let me go without telling anyone. But I knew I had to tell my mother, because sooner or later the truth would probably come out.

When I got home, I told my mother how I'd cut school that day. Her face got really crazy and her eyes were almost poking out of her head. As she yelled at me, she was spitting so much that my sister was wiping off her face like it was raining cats and dogs.

"You are grounded for one whole week with no TV and no electronics," my mother said. "I'll be coming up to your room to take the phone away from you."

An hour later, my mother had calmed down. We started talking about the issue all over again. She told me I still had to do my punishment so I'd learn from my mistakes, but that she was happy I'd told her all by myself.

That's when I realized that Kim really helped me by making me start doing things on my own. Even though she didn't know me that well, she helped make me choose whether or not I wanted to keep giving in to peer pressure.

I decided I wanted to make a change and that no one else could do it for me. It had to start with me. I resolved to stop smoking, drinking, and hanging out with my old friends.

For one whole week, I hung out by myself. Now that I was going to school every day, I didn't see my old friends because they were still cutting. After school I'd go home and watch TV during my free time. I was being a good person, but I got really bored and lonely.

I felt like I was walking through a maze trying to find some new friends. Then, after a week and a half, I met a boy named Peter and a girl named Vicky at a swim meet after school. They both went to my school and were in my swim group.

I started going to their houses to play video games and chilling with them at the movie theater. One time, the three of us had a conversation about being able to tell each other the truth. Even though it felt a little funny saying it, we all admitted that we had cheated on tests before. We knew cheating was wrong, but we all felt good that we shared something with each other.

When I got home, I told my mother how I'd cut school that day.

Peter and Vicky didn't pressure me to skip school, drink, or smoke. We didn't hang out on the street getting in trouble. I was still going to school, getting good grades and perfect attendance and putting a smile on my mother's face.

When we went to the movies, I remembered my old friends sitting next to me. I remembered jumping because we were scared of the movie, with the popcorn going up into the air and getting on the people in front of us—and them thinking we threw it at them. Those were the good old days.

But if I were still listening to my old friends, I would be just like a remote control car, going everywhere they wanted and just being used all the time.

Now when I get pressure from a peer, I deal with it by using my brain.

Recently, one of my classmates asked me to slap another classmate on the back of the head when he was asleep, so no one would know who did it. I told him that if he was so big and bad, he should do it himself.

Now when I get pressure from a peer, I deal with it by using my brain. I go back to my memory of when I messed up with my old friends, and I tell myself I don't want to face those consequences again.

Charlene was 20 when she wrote this story.

Julio Juarez

Hiding My Talent No More

By Jesselin Rodriguez

When I was in elementary school, doing well in school was the only thing that mattered to me. I always thought that being the smartest meant being the best.

I got this idea because when my family used to ask me if I had done my homework and I told them "yes," they would say, "What a good little girl!" Every time they said something like that, it would go straight to my head. It made me feel like I was number one.

In my elementary school, a lot of kids seemed to share my attitude. It was common to see kids always wanting to do their best so that they could be teacher's pet. I would sometimes hear a teacher say to someone else, "Oh, this is so wonderful, you're the best student in the class, I've never had a problem with you." I wanted to hear a teacher say those things to me, too.

When I got to junior high school this all changed. The mood and the atmosphere of the school were totally different from what I was used to. When I walked in there for the first time at the beginning of sixth grade, it seemed like everyone was just chillin'. I saw kids walking in and out of the building like nothing, hanging out in the auditorium when they didn't belong there, and even screaming at teachers. There was a fight almost every day. No one seemed to care about classes.

In that environment, you looked crazy if you were doing any work. The important thing was to have friends. If you didn't have any friends, then you were nothing. You would get picked on, cursed out in the hallways, and if you had a fight it was never be one-on-one. I decided schoolwork wasn't going to be my top priority anymore. Instead, I made it a point to have friends.

*I*nstead of always going to class and doing my homework, like I had in elementary school, I got into a new routine. I started thinking of school as a playground. It was like I could do anything there—cut class, write on the walls, hide in the bathrooms—and nobody would know about it because there were so many kids in that school.

When I did go to class, I'd walk in 20 minutes late, sit with a friend, and talk the rest of the period away. When the teachers would ask me why I was late, I'd tell them that I was in the bathroom or that I was talking to another teacher about something. They wouldn't really bother me after that.

This doesn't mean that I never did any work. I did just enough to pass. But I made it a point never to let my friends find that out. On the days when I did my homework, I used to wait until after the class to give it to the teacher so my friends wouldn't see. If they knew, I was sure they would give me a hard time. They would be like, "What are you doing the work for? What, you think you're better than us?"

It's always been a big thing to me, caring about what other people thought. In elementary school, I was liked and respected for being smart and always doing my work—not just by my family and the teachers but by the other kids too. But in junior high, I thought my classmates would like me better if I acted more like them—lazy and not caring about anything except going home to watch TV.

After pretending to be lazy for a while, I started to get lazy. By January of sixth grade I hated school. I hated the fact that I had to get up so early (and it's not like I had a long trip 'cause I lived right across the street from the school). I hated to do my homework. After class, I just wanted to go to my bed and sleep or watch TV. The less work I did, the harder it got to do any work at all.

I decided schoolwork wasn't going to be my top priority anymore. Instead, I made it a point to have friends.

A lot of my teachers said that I had the potential to get high marks if I spent more time in class and got rid of my friends. But I didn't listen. I thought that they were just saying that. I didn't think that they really cared. When I brought my report card home, my mom would say, "I know you can do better, next time I want this to be higher." I didn't listen to her either.

Then something happened. My class was divided up. The kids with the worst behavior and grades, including most of my friends, were sent to a different class. Since I didn't have my crew to do things with anymore, I had two choices—I could either not come to school at all, or I could start doing my work.

I knew my mother would kill me if she ever heard me say anything about not going to school. So I started to go to class every day and began to do my homework on a more regular basis. My teachers were happy and, inside, so was I.

By the time I was in eighth grade (my last year in junior high), I had worked my way up to a B average. I still felt that I could do better, but I didn't want to get higher grades than most of the people in my class. I thought that they would get mad at me and be like, "Oh, now she thinks that she's smarter than me."

Then came ninth grade and a big reality check. I had thought that high school was going be the same as junior high only more so—a bigger playground to roam in. I was wrong. Even though most of the kids were the same, the atmosphere was very different.

You see, my zoned high school had been closed and several new, smaller schools had been started to replace it. My school was brand new and so small that there were only about 50 students in the whole place. There was no chance to run around because every teacher knew who you were and where you were supposed to be every minute of the day.

Boy, I hated it! I felt so trapped and closed in. I hated that everyone knew who you were. And I hated the fact that I had to do my work because there was no place to hide. If you tried to go to class a little late, your teacher would come and hunt you down. Even though I had started to work a little harder, I still had days when I didn't feel like doing anything. But I could no longer just chill at the back of the class or say that I was going to the bathroom and come back 15 or 20 minutes later. The teachers wouldn't let me get away with it.

My teachers knew that I was smart and saw right through my front of acting like I didn't care. Still, I thought that as long as I handed in a couple of pieces of work where I did my best, they would be satisfied and not bother me all the time. But they wouldn't leave me alone. For my whole freshman year, I was constantly told that I could do better. It just went in one ear and came out the other.

Then, over the summer after ninth grade, I was talking to a friend of mine who was in college. He asked me how I was doing in school. I told him that I was doing OK.

"How OK?" he asked. I told him I was doing just enough to pass. He asked me why, when I could be at the top of my class if I wanted. I told him that I had gotten very lazy.

Then he asked me if I wanted to go to college and I said yes.

What I really wanted was to get a scholarship so that I could go to a college out of state.

My friend started telling me that there was no way I was getting a scholarship the way I was going. Then he told me that I should probably just forget about college because it seemed like I would never even be able to finish high school if I was so lazy.

He put so much fear in me that I spent the rest of that summer thinking about what he said. It was the same thing my teachers had been telling me for years. It finally started to sink in. For a long time, it had been my dream to be the first one in my family to graduate from high school and go to college. Now I realized that I was going to have to work to make that dream come true.

I thought my classmates would like me better if I acted more like them—lazy and not caring about anything.

A week before school started, I promised myself that I was going to bring my grades up until they couldn't get any higher. And that's exactly what I did.

For my whole tenth grade year I did nothing but work. I used to be in school from 8 in the morning until 5:30 or 6 in the evening. I did so well that most people were like, "I knew you had it in you, but I didn't realize how much."

I was staying after school so much that my adviser started to worry about me. The principal even started kicking me out because I was there really late practically every day. (I could never figure out why they were complaining about my staying after school. I thought that was a good thing.)

Breaking my lazy habits wasn't easy. In fact, I think it was the hardest thing I have ever done. I had to get used to doing my homework every night, not just when I felt like it. And I had to make a lot of sacrifices. I couldn't sit home and watch TV all day. I hardly listened to the radio. And I didn't see a lot of my friends outside of school. Every time my friends used to say, "Jesse, let's go downtown so I can go buy this shirt" or "Let's go downtown and just chill," I was always saying "No, I can't, I have to stay after school and finish my work."

I've made a lot of new friends since junior high and I think they're part of the reason why I've been able to change. Because of them, I don't worry so much anymore about what other people will think of me if I get good marks. They accept me the way I am. If they don't see me studying, they will be like, "Why aren't you doing any work? That's not like you. You better hurry up, this is due Friday." That makes me feel good. Because they really care, they want to see me work.

So, here I am, a junior almost ready for college—not at all ashamed of how bright I am, and not caring who knows it. It feels like that good girl I once had inside me has come back.

Jesselin was 16 when she wrote this story.
She later attended Hampshire College.

Matty DeLuna

Why I Speak My Mind

By Desiree Bailey

When I first met Mary in my freshman English class, she looked like a scary teenager in a long black coat with huge chains and crosses hanging from her neck. But as we started talking about school, I started seeing her as a vulnerable girl who put up a wall to protect herself. We became friendly. Some people taunted her about her frightful clothing, but I talked to her whenever I saw her in the hallways.

During sophomore year, I stopped seeing her around school. I didn't think anything of it because our school is so big and over-crowded that sometimes I don't see a friend for weeks. When I finally saw Mary at the library one day, she said she hadn't been in school for a couple of weeks. Instead, she'd been hanging out with her friends at malls and other places.

I laughed to conceal what was running through my mind. I

really wanted to tell her that her friends were trouble and that she should return to school. I was scared for her—nothing good could come out of cutting school for weeks. But I didn't think it was my place to tell her what to do. Besides, I didn't want to offend her, so I said nothing.

I never saw her again. Now, two years later, I've started to wonder if she turned her life around or if she is still spiraling downward.

I wish I'd made some attempt to help Mary resist the urge to cut school. I wish I could have talked her into going back.

But I learned from my experience with Mary. Thinking about my silence back then has made me more willing to speak my mind when it comes to people I care about. When someone I'm close to is doing dangerous things, I tell them frankly what can happen and how I feel about it. I try not to be judgmental, but when the stakes are high, it's hard to hold myself back.

For a while, my 16-year-old friend Lauren was involved with an older guy who had young children. She didn't know who the children's mother was. For all we knew, she could have been a violent woman who could have seriously hurt Lauren. Or she simply could have been protective of her kids and not happy about having some other "woman" around them.

And who was this man anyway? He knew Lauren was 16 and he still got involved with her. Apparently he wanted some type of "friends with benefits" relationship. I was extremely worried for Lauren.

When she said she wanted to buy clothes for the kids, that was the last straw for me. I told Lauren she was too young to be in that situation. All my friends and I tried over and over to talk her out of it. She said she saw the logic in our words, but she continued to see him for a while. After a couple of months, though, Lauren started dating another guy who was closer to our age.

I'm glad I spoke up in Lauren's situation. I think I helped her take a step back and look at what she was doing. But even if she hadn't changed a thing, at least the message would've been in her head. And I'd know that I'd done the best I could.

I don't care if people think I'm closed-minded or cowardly because I say "no" to bad things. I don't believe in doing things that I truly don't want to do, and I don't see the use in harming my body or my future. I look at it as abuse. Why should I let anyone tell me to harm myself? In the end, if something goes wrong, none of those people will be there for me. I will have myself to deal with.

When someone I'm close to is doing dangerous things, I tell them frankly what can happen.

I appreciate it when people respect me enough to accept my decisions. Many times I find they actually want me to remain the way I am. One girl who tried to get me to drink once is also a heavy smoker, and she said she'd kill me if I ever started smoking. Even though she chooses to smoke, she recognizes the dangers and tries to shield me from them.

Peer pressure does exist among my closest friends, but it's positive. If an opportunity comes along, like a scholarship or a great job, we encourage each other to take it.

Though we all have different personalities, some loud, some soft-spoken, we expect certain things from each other. We're all goal-oriented and want to be successful. While we all like to have fun, we know what's truly important, and we push each other to stay on track.

If I'm procrastinating about an essay for school, I'll get to it faster if I learn that one of my friends already did it. My friend's acceptance to MIT (a really good school in Massachusetts) inspired the rest of us to try to follow in his footsteps by paying more attention to applications and scholarships. No one wants to feel left out—even in the group with the top grades.

Peer pressure is like a person with many faces. On the one hand, it reminds me of the old saying "misery loves company."

Those who negatively pressure others just want to drag someone else down with them. And I will not allow anyone to bring me down. On the other hand, when people pressure me to do better, it can be an uplifting force that encourages success.

Desiree was 17 when she wrote this story.
She later attended Georgetown University.

Sex Doesn't Make You a Man

By Damon Washington

I'm 17 years old and proud to be a virgin.

I choose not to have sex because I'm still young and have a lot of life ahead of me. I have college to look forward to and having sex won't help me further my education.

Of course, the idea of having sex does cross my mind every now and then, but I already have too much to deal with in my life as it is. I have goals. I want to get married, become a writer and, if I'm lucky, play football in the pros someday. Having sex will not make these things happen.

Until a couple of years ago I lived in the Cypress Hills Projects in Brooklyn, New York. I experienced everything there—guns, drugs, violence. But a lot of the time the main issue was sex. Outside on the benches my friends always talked about how they were going to get with this girl and that girl. They would call girls nasty names whenever they wouldn't give them the time of day. In fact, I've never seen these guys do anything nice for a girl. To them, they were just sex objects.

My friends would question me constantly about whether I ever "got any."

"No," I'd tell them.

"What's the matter with you?" my friend Kevin asked one time. "You too busy or something?"

"Yeah," I told him. "Because, unlike you guys, I want to treat girls with respect before I even think about moving to the next level."

"Man, you don't know what you missing."

My friends teased me so much that I almost felt I had to have sex just to get them off my back. But no matter how many times they asked me, they still got the same answer: "I'm still a virgin and proud of it." As long as I'm happy with myself and what I've accomplished in life, I don't have to prove anything to anybody.

Two years ago I was in a relationship with a girl named Lynnette. We spent time together, talked on the phone a lot, and showed our affection towards one another by hugging and kissing. One day Lynnette and I were talking and I asked her if she had ever had sex. She said she hadn't. Then she asked me the same question and I told her I hadn't either.

Lynnette told me that in her past relationships sex was all her boyfriends thought about, 24-7. And when she found that out, she dumped them. She said she hoped that I wasn't that type of guy, because she would dump me too. I told her I wasn't and that being with her was all I ever needed.

We used to joke around about sex in terms of who would last the longest, but our relationship was based on having fun together. Lynnette said she wanted to be married before she had sex and I respected her for that. Not too many people our age realize that waiting to have sex can be a good experience.

It's not that I didn't think about it sometimes, or that we didn't have plenty of opportunities. Once Lynnette and I went over to my house after church, and my mother went out and left us all alone. We were talking, kissing, and playing around, acting silly. Then we went to my mother's room to watch a movie. I was still playing around with her but Lynnette seemed more interested in the movie than me and I felt kind of neglected.

As long as I'm happy with myself, I don't have to prove anything to anybody.

After the movie was over we went downstairs to the kitchen. Lynnette was cooking ribs and watching a basketball game on TV. She was a big time Chicago Bulls fan but I wasn't into it. I tried to take Lynnette's mind off the game by kissing her.

"Stop," she said, and kind of pushed me off.

When my mother came home and we took Lynnette home, I didn't say much to her because she'd been ignoring me.

"What's the matter with you?" she asked. "Why aren't you talking to me?"

"Nothing," I said.

I walked her to the door and just when I was getting ready to leave she said, "Hold up. You ain't gonna give me a kiss?" I walked over, kissed her, and went back to my mother's car.

Later that night Lynnette called to find out what the problem was. "Why didn't you want to kiss me when you dropped me off?" she asked.

"Because I didn't like the way you was ignoring me," I said.

"It wasn't like I was ignoring you the whole time," she said. "It's just that you kept kissing on me."

"I have a confession to make," I said. "The reason I kept kissing on you was because I was kind of anxious to take our relationship further, and by us being in the situation we was in, the moment was there and anything could've happened. I was wrong and I'm sorry."

"I forgive you," Lynnette replied. "But it wasn't like I was gonna let you take advantage of me. You should know me better than that."

"I know I should've never thought about you in that kind of way," I said. "I just thought that if we continued to get to know each other like we did, then maybe something could have happened between us."

"Maybe I will have sex someday, but only with my future husband on our honeymoon," she said.

It felt good being honest with Lynnette that day. It showed me that we can overcome any obstacle as long as we are honest with one another.

About six months after we started going out, Lynnette moved to Georgia, but we are still together. Eventually, when we are reunited, we will just pick up where we left off and see where we go from there.

I almost felt I had to have sex just to get them off my back.

The time to have sex will come in the distant future. Hopefully we will be married and make love on our honeymoon.

Sex doesn't make a relationship—it's the love and dignity of how you feel about one another that does. I love Lynnette with all my heart. I was faithful to her. I was there for her through the good and bad times. I was there to console her when she was sick. She once said to me that I filled her heart up with joy, and that is why she wants me to be hers forever.

That may not seem like much to some, but to me it's what a real relationship is all about.

Damon was 17 when he wrote this story.
He went on to attend Brooklyn College.

Alan Arrata

My So-Called Friends

By Sharon Feder

I started high school knowing I needed to make new friends. Again.

Although I hung out with kids in my neighborhood once in awhile, we didn't really connect; I knew them as family friends. I always made my real friends at school.

But because I've gone to seven different schools in my life, it's sometimes been hard to keep those friendships. My relationships with "school friends" never lasted for long after I moved on to my next school.

I'm very friendly, so I usually didn't have trouble starting over in a new school. During the first few weeks of freshman year, I started conversations with lots of different people, including Chris, a guy I recognized from my junior high.

One day when he and I were talking, we were joined by Mike,

another guy from junior high. Mike and I didn't really know each other. He used to hang out with a group of kids who seemed immature.

Once we started talking, though, I found out that Mike and I had a lot in common. We'd both gone to yeshivas (Jewish schools) for elementary school and knew a lot of the same people. We began to hang out. We'd listen to music, talk about what was going on in school, or just sit around and do nothing.

Once we got to know each other better, we started seeing each other outside of school as well. We'd go to each other's houses, watch movies, play basketball and go online. We'd almost always have a good time.

Mike and I hung out with Tara, who sat behind me in Hebrew class. She too had gone to yeshiva and knew people from my old school.

Tara was blunt and usually said what she thought. She'd go up to a complete stranger on the bus and say, "I really like your shoes" or tell a friend that her hair looked awful. She had strong beliefs about politics and religion, which she'd stand up for even if everyone else disagreed. I admired her honesty and enjoyed discussing things with her.

The more I hung out with them, the more I started acting like them. School and good grades mattered less to me.

Even though Mike, Tara and I had a lot in common and felt comfortable with each other, in some ways we were very different.

For one thing, school's a very important part of my life. I want to go to a good college, so I've always taken hard courses and tried to get the highest possible grade in every class. I'm the kind of person who stays after school for extracurricular activities and then goes home to study.

But Mike and Tara saw school as a place they had to go to, not a place they wanted to be. Tara got good grades but didn't put a lot of effort into it; Mike sometimes cut classes and got other people to do his work for him. And once the school day was over, they'd both run out as soon as possible.

Unlike me, Mike and Tara both had good friends outside of school—people they'd known since elementary school. When we first became close, Mike and Tara would divide their free time between our group of three and their old friends.

We'd usually hang out together on Friday night and then I'd spend the rest of the weekend alone at home or going places with my family, while they saw their other friends.

Then, sophomore year, both Tara and Mike started to incorporate their closest friends into our group. Mike brought Boris and Robert and Tara brought Elizabeth, Debbie, and Martha.

Mike, in particular, liked the idea of having a big crowd to hang out with all the time. I didn't like the new people as much as I liked Mike and Tara, but I did like having a more active social life.

We'd all meet after school at least once a week and every weekend we'd go out to dinner or to the movies or sit around at one of our houses watching a video. I always had something fun to do and I got to spend more time with Mike and Tara, even though it wasn't just the three of us.

Although I got along well with almost everyone on a one-to-one level, I felt a little alienated from the group as a whole. Being with their other friends brought out my least favorite sides of Mike and Tara.

Mike's rude, immature streak, which had diminished since junior high, came out in force when Boris and Robert were around. With them, he was more likely to do things I hated, like burp, fart, or make racist and homophobic remarks. And the guys shared interests like wrestling and computers, which I couldn't care less about.

As for Tara, she and her other girlfriends shared the same tastes in music and fashion, which were different from mine.

They were more concerned about their looks than I was. It seemed like whenever they got together, a copy of *Seventeen* or some bridal magazine was also present.

While I dressed pretty conservatively and always thought brand names were a waste of money, the other girls, especially Martha, were really into designer clothing and talking about Gucci this and Gucci that.

I let them influence me—the more I hung out with them, the more makeup ended up on my face. And, even though my clothing remained relatively conservative, a few pricey low-cut shirts made their way into my closet.

When it came to music, I liked everything, from pop to reggae to country, but they only listened to what was on popular stations or to Middle Eastern music, since a few of them were from Israeli families.

I was willing to listen to their music, but whenever I tried to get them to listen to something different that I liked, they refused to let me put it on.

It was the same story when it came to movies. I was terrified of scary movies, so I'd always say, "Whatever you want, as long as it's not scary," and then they'd drag me to the scariest movie they could find. Whoever was sitting next to me would hold down my arms so I couldn't cover my eyes.

Still, I had fun with them. Their music wasn't bad and even though the movies were scary, they were never as scary as I made them out to be.

I did sometimes wonder why I was hanging out with people who were so different from me. But the more I hung out with them, the more I started acting like them. School and good grades mattered less to me and I began to focus on more superficial things like looks.

Whatever happened with the larger group, Mike and Tara and I had a special bond. On my 16th birthday, for example, the two of them surprised me with an assortment of 16 balloons. That was one of the sweetest things anyone's ever done for me. I felt lucky to have such good friends.

But things changed during junior year. I realized that college was coming up and I had to improve my grades. I was still very close to the group, but they didn't seem to appreciate how much stress I was under.

I killed myself working all day and night, and by the middle of the school year I was physically and emotionally exhausted. I continued to spend what little free time I had with them, but I was no longer as willing to put up with attitudes and behavior that I didn't like.

In the past, when someone in the group said something stupid or racist to me, I responded by either giving them a look or a nudge with my arm. Now I unloaded on them, saying very bluntly just how much I hated those comments.

Things started to get tense between us. I was liking most of them less and less and I could tell that they were starting to think the same about me. By the spring of junior year, the only person in the group I really felt close to was Tara.

One day in April, Tara called me and begged me to come over. Mike and Boris were on their way and she said she didn't want to be alone with them. I wasn't in the mood, but decided to go anyhow. Elizabeth went too.

As we sat in Tara's room, Mike and I bickered over stupid things—it was as though we were bored and trying to provoke each other. He'd start with a racist comment or just say something mean, and I'd reply with my opinion, which I did not state very nicely.

At dinner I tried to ignore him and pay more attention to the other people. On the way back to Tara's house from the restaurant, we cranked up the radio in the car and sang along at the top of our voices. At that moment I was really happy, even though the tension between Mike and me was just beneath the surface.

When we got back to Tara's, everyone started joking around. Mike and Elizabeth pretended to fight. I was standing near them and Mike kept falling back on me. I told him to stop, but he kept doing it.

One of his falls squashed my hand against Tara's dresser. I yelled, "Stop! Get away from me!" but he continued pretending to fight with Elizabeth as if nothing had happened. My hand didn't hurt that much but I still left Tara's house very annoyed.

When I woke up the next morning my hand was killing me. My mother joked, "Maybe you have arthritis," but I knew why it hurt. By the middle of the day my hand had started turning purple and I couldn't move it.

I rushed to the doctor thinking that it was broken, but it wasn't. The doctor told me that I had tendonitis—not horrible, but painful. I'd have to wear a brace for a while.

I emailed Mike to tell him what had happened and asked if we could talk about it over the phone. He repeatedly typed "No!" in instant messages. He seemed more concerned about whether I was going to blame him than the fact I was in pain.

That bothered me. I needed him as a friend to say, "Sharon, are you OK?" He didn't.

When I started spending more time on other people's interests than on my own, I wasn't being true to myself.

The next night, dazed on painkillers and feeling alone, I got a phone call. It was Martha, the person in the group I was the least close to.

Martha never seemed interested in anything I had to say. When I was talking about something I cared about, she'd say "Sharon, stop babbling," which hurt my feelings. We didn't talk or see each other outside of the group, so I had no clue why she was calling me.

"Sharon, you're an instigator…a horrible person…you hate everything and everyone…and no one likes you!" she said harshly. She told me that everyone laughed about me when I wasn't around and that I was nothing but "stupid."

I hung up the phone. I felt as though my heart had been pulled from my body. I'd never gotten a call like that. It was the absolute meanest thing anyone has ever done to me. What made it worse was that I was sure that either Mike or his friend Boris had put her up to it. How else would she have gotten my number?

I immediately called Tara and, crying hysterically, told her what had happened. She calmed me down and told me that none of what Martha had said was true.

"That's just what Martha does," she said. She explained that Martha had said similarly mean things to her countless times when they'd fought.

I was disappointed in Tara's response. "Just what Martha does?" I thought. "How could anyone justify someone doing something that horrible?"

If I'd thought Martha was just acting on her own, I would've felt bad, but it wouldn't have hurt as much as it did. But things had gotten so bad between Mike and me that I was sure he had something to do with it.

I was convinced that one of my closest friends had betrayed me and that the other people I'd spent most of the past three years with had turned against me. I felt depressed and alone and I hated it. I cried for the rest of the night.

That was it; I was no longer part of the group. No one was talking to me except Tara. The people who used to call and email me every night had nothing to say to me anymore.

I wanted to call Mike and Boris to confront them, but I didn't feel that I could trust them anymore. I imagined them lying about how Martha got my number and telling me again that Mike hadn't hurt my hand.

My birthday was a week away and I didn't want to face it. Tara and my family offered to celebrate with me, but I said I'd rather not. I was too depressed.

I told Tara that all I wanted for my birthday was balloons. But when I saw her at school, she was empty-handed. She'd forgotten. She wished me a happy birthday and we parted ways.

That night I got a phone call from Mike.

I don't remember exactly what he said, other than wishing me a happy birthday. It was nice that he remembered, but strange that he acted as though nothing had happened between us. When we hung up, it was clear to me that our friendship was over.

I still considered Tara my friend, even though she remained close to the others. I decided that didn't matter. I still wanted to be friends with her and I knew it was unfair to expect her to choose.

But after I stopped hanging out with the rest of the group, Tara seemed distant. We'd always gotten together every day before school to talk; suddenly that changed.

Tara met me less and less, and when she did, she didn't talk very much. We stopped seeing each other outside of school. On Saturday nights she was still going out with the group, while I was at home by myself.

I remembered how Tara had begged me to come over the day all the trouble started, because she didn't want to be alone with the very people that she now seemed to be choosing over me. I was confused and angry.

When I told Tara I wanted to know whether or not she was still my friend, she acted surprised. She told me that of course we were still friends. But she wasn't acting like it. I made an effort to keep our friendship going, but she never called me or returned my calls.

With time, I was able to get over the whole mess. I was busy with different school activities. And friends and acquaintances I hadn't seen for a long time reappeared to comfort me when they heard what had happened.

I reconnected with Jeff, a close friend from junior high; it felt great talking to him again. I realized that he was a true friend, making sure I was all right and willing to take me back after I'd stopped talking to him for so long. He helped me get through my hard time.

In a way, I'm grateful for what happened because it taught me the people in the group were not the right friends for me.

They say opposites attract, but my ideas and goals were too different from theirs. I'm not the stereotypical just-want-to-have-fun teenager. I'm more interested in accomplishing as much as I can and leaving a mark.

Being part of the group was fun for a while, and maybe I needed to prove to myself that I could have a social life that didn't revolve around studying and extracurricular activities. But I should've realized when I started spending more time on other people's interests than on my own that I wasn't being true to myself.

I don't know who I'll be friends with at school this year and I don't know how I'll handle it when I see Tara and Mike there, but it doesn't scare me. I'm happy with what I have now, even though my social life isn't what it used to be.

I do miss the friendship I once had with Mike and Tara, as well as the days of automatic weekend plans with a crowd of people. But I wouldn't go back. I know that I have a great year ahead of me—prom, graduation, getting ready for college—and I can't wait!

Sharon was 17 when she wrote this story.
She later graduated from college with a degree in journalism.

Lee Samue

Making Me Dance

By Jill Feigelman

"Auditions are Friday at 4 p.m.," said Ms. Napolitano, my dance teacher. She was announcing auditions for the high school's dance company in my 5th period dance class. I knew she was directing her comments at me. She seemed to expect I'd join.

I've been dancing since I was about 3 years old. I used to say I was going to be a dancer and a doctor when I grew up. Sometimes when I'm dancing I get too busy thinking about other things to just dance and be in the moment. But when I'm focused, it feels relaxing and fun.

I loved the idea of joining my school's dance company, which performs at school assemblies and the annual dance concert in June. But I thought there was no way I could do it. I was too busy my sophomore year, struggling in chemistry and studying for the statewide math exam.

But if I knew I couldn't do it, why did I keep questioning myself? Why did I keep asking my mom if I should try out? What superpowers did Ms. Napolitano have over me to keep my brain trying to figure out how to fit dance into my schedule? Maybe like Spider Man, she had bitten me with a "gotta dance" spider. As if Ms. Napolitano weren't bad enough, my friends started telling me to join.

C ome on," said my friend Jackie, a member of the dance company. "You're a good dancer. You like dancing and it's good for college."

"Jill, try out," said my friend Teona, another member of the dance company. "It's fun. You'll make it."

After defeating the "gotta dance" bug, I finally said "no" to the pressure to dance. But when my friend Olivia and I went to the dance show last June, I felt like I should have been up there dancing. And when junior year rolled around, so did Jackie and Teona, chanting, "Join, join, join."

Even though I expected junior year to be even harder than sophomore year, something inside me said "Audition."

I felt really happy when I made it—despite the fact my

I was happy my friends had kept bugging me to join. Their positive peer pressure pushed me to do something I really loved.

last name was spelled wrong on the dance list. The unofficial dance captain, who I didn't know, saw me looking at the names and said, "You're Jill, cool." She made me feel like I was already part of the team.

But getting on the team increased the pressure. How would we get our jazz piece done in three weeks? I should drop out. I mean I couldn't do it. I had an AP American history project due the next day.

But I didn't drop out—and I was so glad to get back on stage in December for our jazz performance. I could see my mom in the audience and my fellow dancers smiling. We made some mistakes but it was pretty good. Everyone clapped and cheered a lot, and it felt good to be the center of attention.

I was happy my friends had kept bugging me to join because I needed their encouragement. Their positive peer pressure pushed me to do something I really loved.

Sometimes it's hard to juggle all of my schoolwork and other activities, but I'm so glad to be a member of the company. Now I'm convinced that if I want to do something and I can't get it out of my head, I should give it a shot.

Jill was 16 when she wrote this story. She enrolled in the journalism program at Syracuse University.

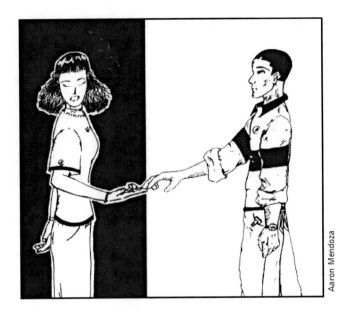

Aaron Mendoza

Peer Pressure Ended Our Relationship

By Lenny Jones

Dear Maggie,

I know I'm probably the last person on earth that you want to hear from, but I'm writing you this letter to apologize for the way I treated you, to explain why I did the things I did, and to set things straight. So sit back and relax—it's going to be a long ride.

About three years ago (before I met you), I remember hearing a lot about the controversy of interracial dating from my friends and on TV talk shows. (On every show, there's some Afrocentric woman yelling from the crowd that black men shouldn't go outside their race, because black women have all that they would ever need. If not that, there's some white girl's mother protesting against an interracial relationship because she claims a black boyfriend beat on her daughter.)

But I didn't really care about all the controversy. I thought that if two people loved each other (you and I, for instance), race didn't matter. But that was before we started dating.

About two summers ago, when we first met at your mother's house, I thought you were cool and everything. You were Jewish but not that religious. I guess that was just the way your family brought you up. Anyway, we seemed to hit it off pretty well.

As we got to know each other better, you ended up being my first girlfriend of a different race. I didn't see anything wrong with it. You were just like any other girl and you pretty much acted like one, too (that's a good thing, by the way).

The only problem was all the negative reaction from friends and perfect strangers. They called me a sellout for going out with "white trash." One time this old black lady saw us and called me a "volunteer slave." The criticism bothered me a lot and it kind of gnawed its way through our relationship.

Another problem was that I was thinking of joining the Nation of Islam because I felt a sense of unity with my brothers and sisters, and some of the Nation's beliefs I can agree with. (All those other religions never really interested me—I felt that a lot of those so-called "Servants of God" who taught from the Bible were full of b.s. and only out for the money.)

The thought of joining the Nation of Islam became bigger and bigger as our relationship went on. But there was one big problem—a friend told me that the Nation prohibited interracial dating.

Because of my inability to communicate (what do you expect—I'm a guy), our relationship kept getting weaker and weaker. I never told you about all the problems I was dealing with. I hid my feelings and went on like nothing was wrong.

The things people were saying really started to sink into my head. I started to ask myself, "Am I really a sellout?" and "Am I really so desperate I have to go out with a white girl?"

I was really self-conscious when I went out with you in

public. Whenever we left your mostly white neighborhood and went to the movies, traveled on the train, or went anywhere in Brooklyn, I felt like everybody was staring at me. I could imagine what they were saying to themselves: "Damn, why does he have to bring that around here?"

I was so scared of what people might say that I didn't want to be seen in public with you. Whenever we went out, you always wanted to hold hands (which I usually really liked). But when we were in a mostly black neighborhood or when a group of black people walked by, I tried to get you to let go of me with stupid excuses like,

I thought that if two people loved each other, race didn't matter. But that was before we started dating.

"My wrist is hurting," or, "I got arthritis," and I played it off like I didn't even know you. Then you would want to hold the other hand and I would make even stupider excuses like, "If one hand hurts, the other may too," or, "My hand fell asleep."

I know that my excuses probably bothered you a lot (although not as much as they bothered me), but you would wait a while and then ask me, "Did your hand wake up yet?" You never told me that I hurt your feelings and I never asked.

Another problem was that you lived upstate and I only saw you every other week. When you weren't around, I was hearing a lot of negative things from my nation friends, like, "She's a devil," "Stay with your own people," and "Keep away from those white people. They're just trying to control you."

Other friends who thought they were so smart (yet always failed history class) gave me history lessons. They told me that I was disrespecting Malcolm X and his faith at the same time I was trying to join it. They also talked about how white people enslaved us for hundreds of years and how blacks lost their lives in wars so that we could be free and, in return, I was just spitting on their graves.

I thought a lot about what they were saying, Maggie, and

I began to despise you. I thought a lot more about joining the Nation. The more I saw you, the more I hated you because of what your ancestors did to mine. Everything you did annoyed me for no reason.

And the weirdest thing of all is that whenever I was at your house, you always wanted to watch Spike Lee's film about Malcolm X (your favorite movie). Here I was, trying not to let racism ruin our relationship, and there you were, watching a three-hour movie about a black nationalist leader.

Watching the movie forced me to think about every negative thing that was said about our relationship. When the movie ended you'd sit there and smile, while I sat there pissed off.

But what really surprised me was that your family treated me with the utmost respect. They didn't give me any strange looks or nasty comments. They treated me like one of the family and in return I feel like I stabbed them in the back. I feel ashamed.

Unfortunately, when it came to my own family, I was too paranoid and afraid to tell them that we were going out. Remember the time we went on that family picnic and I decided to bring you along? I didn't want to tell

I was so scared of what people might say that I didn't want to be seen in public with you.

my family that we were going out. I told them we were just friends, and I made sure you didn't make any "beyond friendly" contact with me.

I didn't really want to know how my family felt, since I was the first in the family (that I know of) to be in an interracial relationship. And when one person knows something in my family, the whole family knows.

Anyway, our relationship continued while I was practicing to join the Nation of Islam. I stopped eating pork, tried to fast for 30 days (I'm skinny enough already—if I didn't eat for a month, I might have disappeared!), and prayed to Allah (the Muslim God).

Now it was time for me to choose between a religion that I felt comfortable with or being with someone who truly loved me.

Unfortunately, I made the wrong choice. I decided to go with the religion.

So I stopped taking your phone calls and wouldn't call you back. I basically stayed away from you and made up excuses. I told you I was on restriction or I made you think that I thought you were cheating on me (which I knew you didn't do). During this whole ordeal, I felt my heart constantly snapping apart and I was getting depressed. I turned a beautiful experience into something horrible and distasteful.

Remember the time when you called me and I got a friend to answer and tell you that I was with another girl? I basically treated you like crap. I just wanted you out of my life and didn't really care about your feelings. Now I regret everything I did to you, but I guess I can't change the past. I can only learn from it.

During the time that I spent alone, without you, I was able to think about the turn of events that led to our breaking up and how I treated you. I was so worried about my reputation that I totally separated myself from you and everything you had to offer. We could have had a picture perfect relationship, but I had to go and screw it up.

The funny thing is that the "friends" who told me everything that was wrong with you (even though they never met you) hadn't had a monogamous relationship in who knows how long (and from the way they were going, wouldn't have one any time soon).

You also made me realize how much of a follower I am and how much I need to be accepted. I never really hated you, but I let people make me believe that I should. I feel really stupid about what I did and wish I could tell you I'm sorry face-to-face, but I know that will never happen and I have to deal with it. But if you're reading this now, I sincerely apologize for my behavior.

I treated you like a nobody and I guess you got the picture

because after a while you never called or wrote me again.

I was so depressed not hearing from you that I gave up the idea of joining the Nation. I realized I didn't feel comfortable not being able to date whoever I wanted to. The religion that I was about to join was trying to change me.

Because of religion and society's attitudes I lost someone very special, and I will never have your heart again. I know about all the stuff done by white people in the past, but I'm not going to let ignorance or racism destroy any future relationships.

If anything, you made me open my eyes to the racism that was in me and all of us. Maggie, you shouldn't have gone through all the stuff I put you through, but what's done is done and I'm ready to learn from my mistakes.

Love (I hope),

Lenny

Lenny was 18 when he wrote this story. As a researcher for travel books, he has traveled extensively around the world.

James Faber

My Bad

By V.P.

It all began when my friend approached me and asked me if I wanted to get some money.

I said, "Where?"

He said, "Robbing houses."

At first I was like, "I don't know," because I didn't like taking people's things and I had never been in trouble before. But then I decided to do it. I thought it might make me more popular on the block. Besides, he was doing it, and at that time I was a follower.

I knew my friend (I'll call him Tom) from playing basketball. People on the block thought Tom was cool because he did bad stuff, like cut school, and he knew how to fight. I also thought he was cool.

I was 12 and Tom was 14, but he acted more mature that his age. He only fought if someone was messing with him. But when he did fight, he almost always won. The older kids on the block treated him the way they would treat somebody their own age.

At the time I was a kid who followed when other kids were doing bad, like cursing and acting a fool. But I was still pretty good. My aunt was a strict person on me, so after school I'd go home and do my homework. I'd do the things my aunt said to do, like sweep and clean my room.

But there was pressure on me to act cool, because we had just moved to that neighborhood and this was a block where kids smoked and acted a little tough. I wanted to fit in, and I thought acting bad was the way to do it. That's why I decided to go along with Tom.

When we went to rob the house, I felt so scared. The apartment was on the fourth floor and we entered through the fire escape. It only took us a couple of minutes to reach the top, but the whole time we were climbing the stairs I was nervous. There was a lot of noise down on the street, like car horns going off. I thought someone might see us.

I was relieved when we got in the apartment. It was a nice home, with pictures of flowers on the wall. Then Tom started putting change from a bottle into his coat pocket, and I got scared again because he was making a lot of noise. Things were falling and hitting the floor hard.

I started helping Tom. Mainly we just took a bunch of change. Then we left and split the money. I only got $5. It wasn't much, but I was happy to have some money in my pocket.

Later on, Tom and I saw some guys coming toward us who were big on the block. They asked us where we were coming from and we told them we had just robbed a house. I thought they'd think we were cool.

But they were just like, "Yeah, right." We didn't want to prove ourselves that much, so we just kept on walking.

While we walked, I felt a little nervous. I wondered, "Did anybody see us?" But mainly I was smiling and thinking, "I'm a big deal now because I robbed a house."

A couple of days later Tom asked me if I wanted to rob another house and I said yes. I thought, "We did it the first time, we can do it again." This time I took my brother with me. We were standing in the apartment putting change in our pockets when the cops came in through the fire escape.

I was in shock. I never thought we would get caught. The cops said to us: "Get on the ground before this gun goes off."

I was on the floor shaking. I really thought the gun was going to go off. And when they took us outside, there was a whole crowd looking at us. All those people saw me with handcuffs on and they looked shocked, probably because I was so small. I thought there might be a friend or family member in the crowd looking at me. I felt ashamed.

They placed me in the car and said they were taking me to the precinct. I thought they were going to put me in jail with some big kids, like kids who would rape me or beat me. (Luckily they didn't.)

When we got to the precinct, they called my house and my aunt came over. She was crying. She was saying, "Why did you do this to me after all I did for you?" I felt like crying with her. I felt bad. I felt that she was right.

People on the block thought Tom was cool because he did bad stuff.

Tom's mother took him home, but my aunt decided not to take my brother and me home because she was so mad. When she left, I felt like going crazy. I felt like breaking something and yelling, but I couldn't because I was in the precinct.

Then the cops gave us some french fries and burgers to eat. They were not harsh with us. They were calm. Then they took me and my brother around, asking us which apartment we robbed. After that, they called my aunt and convinced her to take us back. (We would be on probation.)

For two days my aunt was so mad she didn't talk to us, and

we weren't allowed out of the house. On the third day she let us go outside. You would think that after all I'd been through I would never get in trouble again. But that's not how it happened.

Somehow we forgot the time, and we didn't come back until 11 at night (our curfew was at 10). I thought my aunt would yell and put us on punishment, like no going outside or watching TV.

But I guess part of me really didn't think the punishment would be too bad. After all, nothing that bad had happened after we robbed those houses, and all that we had done this time was be a little late. If I knew that I was going to end up in foster care placement, I definitely would have come in on time. I never thought my aunt was going to call the cops on us.

There was pressure on me to act cool. I wanted to fit in, and I thought acting bad was the way to do it.

The cops were already there when we came home because my aunt had thought something bad had happened. They said that we were bad kids because our aunt gave us another chance and we didn't come in until we felt like it. I wanted to tell my aunt what happened, to explain that it was just a mistake, but the cops were already there so I couldn't talk to her.

The next day my aunt said she wanted us out of the house and social workers from the child welfare agency came and took us away. The worst part was when I found out my brother and I were going to be separated. I was sent all the way upstate. I was so mad. Mainly I was mad at myself for getting in this trouble.

The first few days upstate at a residential treatment center were terrible. I hated when staff yelled and when I got privileges taken away. I was also mad at my aunt. I kept asking, "Why would she do this?" But I also loved her, so I called her as soon as I got to the placement.

The first phone calls we hardly talked. We were just like hi and bye. But after a while my aunt started to explain why she did what she had done. She said, "V., I put you in foster care because I wanted you to do better and I wanted to help you out." I believed her, and I started not being that mad.

We began to see each other on the weekends and it felt good to be with her again. I wanted to get out of that placement so I started doing what I had to. I followed all the rules, and I've done well in school. In September I was discharged and went home.

I'm not glad about the time that I've been in foster care. Sometimes I think I could have learned my lesson by getting on strict punishment at home with my aunt. Then I wouldn't have had to go through some of the hardest things about being in foster care—particularly being away from home so long. It hurts to be away from my aunt. I love my aunt and she takes care of me.

But I'm glad I didn't get a harder punishment. If they had sent me to a juvenile detention center I would have been afraid, and I think all I would have learned is to be scared and angry. In a jail you might get hurt, and there probably wouldn't be too many people around to look out for you. But the people in my group home, like my staff and my social worker, cared about me.

And I've definitely learned my lesson being in foster care. If I stayed in my neighborhood, I think I might have started to get in trouble again—not robbing, but maybe doing things like graffiti. My friends would have influenced me. I would have thought that in order to be down I'd have to be bad. Now I know there are a lot more important things than being cool.

Since my aunt put me in foster care, I've learned to appreciate how good I had it. Now my aunt tells me, "I'm proud of you." Now that I'm home, I'm going to do everything she tells me.

The writer was in high school when he wrote this story.

Guillermo Mata Jr.

The Pastor's Daughter

By Natalia Tavarez

I was raised in a Pentecostal Christian family that attended church three times a week, and my dad is now the pastor of our church. Until 6th grade, I felt like I had a protective barrier shielding me from all outside evil. But when I entered junior high school I was in for a big change.

That was when I began to meet classmates who drank and smoked cigarettes and weed. I overheard conversations at lunch about how this guy got stoned and that girl couldn't stop throwing up at Friday night's party. I'd pretend I was interested in my lunch or I'd try to change the subject. But inside I felt sad. I didn't really know what alcohol or marijuana was, but I knew they were bad for you. I was afraid for my classmates.

In high school, things just got worse. Students would show up with liquor in water bottles and be drunk by first period. In class, they were joined by the happy, funny, red-eyed kids who smoked weed before school. I couldn't believe what was happening, and that some of these people were my friends.

My parents and my church had taught me that this body is just a loan until we go to heaven, so we must treat it with dignity and respect, and not mess it up with booze and drugs.

Everyone knew me as the pastor's daughter, but that didn't stop my friends from criticizing and pressuring me. When I told them "no" and explained why, they called me a "holy-holy" and told me I needed to enjoy life instead of all that church stuff.

> *When I'd tell them no and explain why, they called me a 'holy-holy.'*

Sometimes I was curious to know what was so good about it, why kids were willing to risk suspension to have a smoke, but I never had the nerve to try it. I'd done my share of rebelling, but staying away from drugs and alcohol was something I felt strongly about. I'd go home and feel so confused. Was I supposed to just go to school every day and pretend not to see what was going on, or should I stand out and let my voice be heard?

My question was finally answered one Sunday morning during freshman year, at my church bible class. My teacher announced that we'd be learning about a new subject— peer pressure.

She told us we'd be tempted by things like sex, drugs, and alcohol, but that we must resist and be an example to others. I realized that I wasn't wrong for being different and for not wanting to do what my friends were doing. I felt like a weight had been lifted off me, that I could resist and be that example for my friends.

The next day at school I remembered what my bible teacher had told me. The lunch bell rang and my heart raced as I walked downstairs to the cafeteria. I could see the group of usual characters at my table, and I began to dread it.

By the time I had my brownish, burnt pizza in my hand and walked to the table, my friends were already wrapped up in their conversation. "Yeah, that party was amazing. I couldn't believe Susan's parents weren't home," said Jessica. "And they had cool drinks."

"Yup, and we all know who was having a great time in the back room," said Kimberly, causing all the girls to laugh knowingly.

"Natalia, why didn't you come to the party? You missed out on everything," said Jessica, glaring. "Come to think of it, you're always missing out."

This was it, my moment to let them know how I felt. "I wasn't there because I believe what you guys are doing is wrong, and I want no part in it," I said. My friends looked shocked as I continued. "I don't care if you tease me or call me a holy-holy. I don't want to do things just because you guys are doing them. It's wrong, and you guys should stop."

I breathed a sigh of relief and, shaking, looked down at my food. I had done it. They looked at me, at each other, and then changed the topic. I went home feeling confident that I'd done the right thing.

I promised myself that night that, no matter what, I would remain pure for God. I would be clean—no drugs, no alcohol. After that I stopped hanging out with anyone who tried to pressure me or make me feel bad about not drinking or doing drugs.

Some of my friends have stopped using drugs and I like to believe that my words that day helped them. I still have friends who smoke and drink, and all I can do is remind them of what I believe when they come to me for advice. I've learned that no matter how much I care about them, I need to let them live their own lives, and know that I tried my best to help.

Natalia was 17 when she wrote this story.

Steven Mattor

I Wanted to Be Pretty and Popular

By Sabrina Rencher

As a freshman, I thought that I wasn't beautiful enough for people to like me at my high school. That was difficult to deal with because I wanted to be popular.

I'm originally from Haiti. There, I felt gorgeous. I felt as if I didn't have to do anything to fit in with people at school. We had to wear uniforms, which meant we didn't worry about who was more stylish.

I didn't have to worry about being popular because I'd spent six years in the same school and more than enough students knew who I was.

But once I arrived in the U.S. at age 11, I began to feel insecure. My cousin would talk about stars like Mariah Carey and Jennifer Lopez, saying how beautiful they were and that she wished she had their kind of body.

Back in Haiti, girls my age didn't really go on about the bodies of stars. But after listening to my cousin, I began to think about how I looked. I wasn't sure if I was as sexy or beautiful as these stars.

I also felt insecure because my cousin was thinner than me, which was devastating. I wanted to have the same kind of body she and her friends had.

Sometimes when I looked in the mirror, I saw one of the ugliest girls in the world. Ever since I was little, I'd been getting bumps on my face from eating peanut butter and chocolate. My doctor said it was an allergic reaction.

I started to carry a mirror in my book bag to look at the pretty face that I'd created.

I tried to stop eating these foods but I couldn't help myself. When I had these bumps, my mother sometimes said that my face looked ugly, which made me sad. It hurt my feelings to hear that from my mother.

My looks were still an issue when I started 9th grade. But instead of wanting to have my cousin's body, I wanted to look like the Spanish-speaking girls there. I thought they were beautiful.

Around half of the students at my high school were Latina. It was mostly the Latina girls who wore very tight pants, and some had belly-showing shirts. Many of the other girls covered their bodies, particularly if they were Muslim.

I thought the Latina girls' styles made them look very sexy. Some of them had the body that I dreamed of having. They had almost the perfect butt and chest size. They had slim hips and beautiful faces.

Their hair was longer than mine and looked soft. Some of them also liked to wear lipstick and eye shadow. Since I didn't feel beautiful, I wanted to have their look.

A particular group of Latina girls was well known in the

school. When I first saw them, I thought that they were popular because of their style and because they had the attitude of girls who like to have fun. And since, in my eyes, they were the most beautiful girls in the school, I thought that the only way a girl could be popular was if she was pretty too. I didn't realize the other reason for the Latina girls' popularity was because the school was mostly Spanish-speaking.

I envied them. I was jealous because I wanted to be surrounded by so many friends. I was already friends with some Haitian girls I'd known from junior high. But some of them would talk about me behind my back and create drama. So I felt I'd be happier if I made new friends.

I wanted to befriend the Latina crew. I wanted to get to know them not only because of their looks and popularity, but because they were older and seemed to treat each other with respect. (Of course, I had no way of really knowing this.)

I wanted to be one of them so much that I decided not to eat some of the things that I knew could make me gain weight, like McDonald's, pizza or any other junk food, for a whole month. I also stayed away from peanut butter and chocolate to prevent the bumps.

I started going to a gym near my house to work out every weekend. Then one day, a month after I started to go to the gym, I made another change. I bought lipstick, eye shadow, face powder, lip liners and eyeliners. I went home and gave myself a makeover. I put on my tight jeans and belly-showing T-shirts.

I looked new. I looked like the kind of person who lots of people would think of as beautiful.

I was satisfied. I started to carry a mirror in my book bag to look at the pretty face that I'd created. That's when I started to call myself "Sabrina the Princess." As a result, I felt stronger and more confident.

But my mother didn't like what I'd done to myself. Every time I wore one of my shirts, she said "You are going to wear something over that, right?" I would say "yes" and leave with a shirt closed over my midriff. Then, when I got to school, I'd open it.

But I was still the same person, and I didn't like that. I was quiet around anyone I met, so I decided to change my attitude, too. I thought the only way to be popular was to be like the Spanish-speaking kids, who seemed very outgoing.

So I gave my attitude a little touch up and started acting like the popular Latina crew. I started to look tough and walk sexy. Still, not many people talked to me.

I did make some new friends because they were in my class. But I wanted to be friends with the most popular Latinas because I wanted everybody in school to know who I was.

I spent the rest of 9th grade trying to connect with those girls. I sometimes sat next to them in English or social studies class. But they would say nothing to me. I tried to start conversations with them by saying "Hi." They said, "Oh, hi." And that was it. I had no clue what would work to get them to acknowledge me.

I was upset and didn't know how to handle my feelings. So my sweet self started to change into the kind of person I never had wanted to become. I started to not do my homework. I also started to ignore my mother when she was talking to me.

During the summer after 9th grade, I thought a lot about what happened. I remembered when I was 10 and knew I was coming to America. My uncle was worried that I would become too Americanized, so I made a promise that I wouldn't change myself in order to be liked.

I thought about that promise as I wrote down my thoughts in my journal. I felt horrible about how I was acting because I wasn't listening to my true feelings. But making friends was more important to me than anything else. And I thought to make friends I had to change who I was.

Then one morning in September, before the fall semester started, I turned on the TV and began to watch a talk show. It was about girls who wanted to be popular so badly that they tried to make themselves thinner. They would spend days without eating. Their mothers were worried about them, so they asked the talk show host for help.

The talk show host gave the girls advice that I also needed to hear. He said, "Don't try so hard to be popular in school. If you want to be popular, just be yourself and if the kids don't like you as you, then they don't deserve your friendship."

That made me think about what I was trying to do. Then I realized that I had to be Sabrina. I had to be happy with who I was and not change myself for anybody. That same day, I wrote in my journal about what the talk show host had said and what it meant to me.

My sweet self started to change into the kind of person I never had wanted to become.

I wrote: "Changing myself to fit in a certain crowd is not what I want to do. My mother always taught me how to respect myself and this time I didn't.

"I disrespected myself by thinking that they'd become my friends if I changed my looks and the way I act. I don't have to change myself for them to like me."

I soon returned to school to start 10th grade. The girls I wanted to be friends with last year were in some of the same classes as me. I decided to show them the real me—the Sabrina who is sweet and funny and doesn't obsess about how she looks.

In math class, for instance, I started helping them by explaining problems they didn't understand. That made it easier for us to start talking about other things, like boys!

Eventually, as we got to know each other better, we started going to the mall to hang out and buy stuff that we didn't need, like sunglasses and clothes. We soon became good friends.

We now tell each other secrets and help each other with our homework. We laugh at each other's jokes. I feel like I belong and that they're going to be some of my best friends for a long time, no matter where they are.

I've also become popular in school by just being myself. Before, I thought that if the Spanish-speaking crew were my friends, everybody else would know who I was.

But I'm pretty well known among both students and staff members by interacting with them on my own, rather than just being automatically known as one of the popular girls. (Doing your work and having a sense of humor helps.)

I still wear makeup and belly button showing tops, but not as much as I used to. And I've gone back to eating chocolate and peanut butter despite my bumps. My appearance right now doesn't matter as much to me. I love myself for who I am.

I always go back to read old journal entries. When I get to the page where I wrote about what the talk show host said about changing who you are to fit into the popular crowd, I realize I never want to go back to that planet again.

Sabrina was 15 when she wrote this story.

Jamaal Pascall

The Trouble with Being a Virgin

By Anonymous

Ever since we were kids, my friends Susan, Amaryllis, and I used to hang out three or four times a week and call each other every night to catch up on what we did that day. We were mad close—like sisters.

In junior high, there were times when Susan and Amaryllis would cut out of school. I hardly ever joined them, but the few times I did we went to the movies or to Manhattan to just walk around, bug out, and act silly. I was always the "innocent" one, though. When my friends were experimenting with pot I backed off. Whenever they offered me a forty, I would say "No thanks."

That was my choice. But I didn't think less of my friends if they chose to do something different, and they always respected the fact that I wasn't down with that.

The summer before we entered high school, I went to Puerto Rico on vacation. When I came back, I started hearing a lot of rumors about Amaryllis and Susan sleeping around. I didn't believe them. People were always saying stuff about them and none of it was ever true. So why should I start paying attention to rumors now? I didn't even feel it was worth mentioning.

But once we started high school, things started to change between us. We would only chill once a week. We rarely called each other anymore either, and when we did the conversations always felt incomplete. It was like there was a big area in their lives that I wasn't being filled in on. It seemed they were acting differently whenever I was around.

One day Amaryllis and Susan cut school and wouldn't tell me where they went. It was like this big secret. Another time I was walking with Amaryllis around my block when we ran into Joey, the local flirt. My friends and I always kept away from him, but this time Joey stopped Amaryllis and told her to give him a hug or else he would shout her out. Amaryllis looked real scared and said OK, but warned him not to touch her butt. (Of course he touched her anyway.)

I was confused. "Did I just miss something here?" I asked as soon as Joey finally left her alone. "Since when do you give a hug to Joey?" Amaryllis got really pale and didn't even want to look at me. I dropped it, but I didn't forget.

Then two weeks after that, Amaryllis and Susan were at my house and we were talking about the guys on the block and how stupid they were. "Yeah, remember that day with Joey and Charlie," said Susan. Amaryllis opened her eyes real wide to let Susan know that she just blew their spot.

What happened that day?" I asked.
They looked at each other as if trying to decide whether or not to tell me.

"Forget it," I said, annoyed. "I don't want to know." And I left the room. I was getting sick and tired of all the secrecy.

They followed me, sat me down, and explained to me that it was very difficult for them to tell me because they felt embarrassed. They told me about how, over the summer, they had lost their virginity. I wasn't too surprised—I already knew something was up.

Susan and Amaryllis also told me that, on the day they cut school and didn't want to tell me where they were, they had gone to Joey's house and had sex with him and his friend Charlie. Amaryllis was looking at the floor when she told me. She seemed embarrassed, but Susan was just chilling like it was nothing.

I had to figure out a way to be a virgin and not be a virgin at the same time.

I didn't think differently of them, because they were my friends. But I told them that they made a big mistake. Now Joey had something to bother them with if they ever ignored him, which was really bad news. He could harass them and they would have to do whatever he said unless they wanted to be shouted out and have their names dragged on the floor.

Even though I didn't say it, I was really disappointed in them. When we were kids, all three of us were raised with that law of morality that said you save your virginity until you are married. I always figured we all would abide by it, but apparently I was wrong.

I also knew they didn't even like Charlie and Joey. "I just wanted to see how it would be like," Susan told me. It was a one-time thing and that is really low. I felt my best friends deserved better.

I didn't tell them that, though, because I know not everyone thinks like I do. To Amaryllis and Susan, relationships and even male friendships meant having sex. The way they go about things is different.

Now that my best friends had told me they weren't virgins like me anymore, all the pieces of the puzzle began to fit together.

But, somehow, we were still drifting apart. It was awkward because they were the only ones that I felt comfortable talking to about personal stuff. My other friends in school were cool, but we didn't go back far enough for them to gain my trust. Suddenly, I felt really alone.

One day after school, Susan, Amaryllis, and I were walking to the park. "Remember when we were in junior high and we used to go to the park all the time to chill with everyone," said Susan.

"Yeah," I snapped. "That was when we were close. We used to do everything together, but now we're drifting apart."

"It's different now, that's all," said Amaryllis. "We're changing. We're not in junior high anymore."

"Whatever," I responded.

"It is different," said Susan. "You are a great friend. But for some reason it's like we feel inferior to you. You are always getting high grades, while we barely pass. Even when we chill, you don't like doing anything we like to do."

"We can't talk about sex to you," Amaryllis added. "It's uncomfortable. We don't want to feel like we're talking to a priest."

I just kept saying, "Whatever" until we got to the park. Then I told them, "We've been through so much. Everyone in the whole world can call you 'sluts' but I would never think that way."

After that, we never spoke about our friendship coming apart again, but for weeks I was thinking about what they had said. Then I started noticing that something was wrong with Amaryllis. In class, she was quiet and would put her head down on the desk, which was weird because she was usually laughing and talking to everyone.

I asked her what was the matter, but she said it was nothing. I didn't believe her, but I understood that she felt uncomfortable telling me. I figured it had something to do with her boyfriend.

If I wanted to know what was wrong with her, I had to do something. And I sensed that what stood in the way was me being a virgin. Now I wasn't about to go out and lose my virginity to anybody just like that because my friends were drifting away from me. I had to figure out a way to be a virgin and not be a virgin at the same time.

A few weeks later, I made the decision that I was going to have a long talk with each of my friends and tell them I had sex with Danny, my boyfriend in Puerto Rico, over the summer. I wondered if it would make a difference, if that was the real reason we were drifting apart. I was also curious to see if I could go through with the lie.

I told Amaryllis first. We were in our English class and had to work in pairs. Amaryllis and I finished our work and started talking. "You know," I said. "There's something I haven't mentioned to you about Danny. Remember him?"

"Yeah, of course," she said. "You wouldn't stop talking about him for weeks when you came back from Puerto Rico. Did he come to New York?"

"No. It's something that happened when I was in Puerto Rico with him," I began telling her. "The day before I came back home, Danny took me to the beach. We had mad fun that day. Before he took me to my aunt's house, he took me to his apartment. We were making out on the couch, then things went a little further."

"What do you mean, 'Things went a little further'?" Amaryllis asked with a weird look on her face.

"I lost my virginity to Danny," I blurted out. I almost ruined my whole lie because I could feel myself beginning to laugh, but I managed to hold it in.

"I don't believe you," Amaryllis said. "You and Danny? Nah."

"I didn't want to tell anyone because I wanted to keep it to myself," I responded.

As soon as I convinced her that I wasn't a virgin, Amaryllis told me what was wrong with her. She said that her period hadn't come in over two months and she was feeling real sick. She was scared.

My first thought was that she was pregnant. I immediately

called a women's clinic I had heard about, made an appointment for Amaryllis, and went with her.

It turned out she wasn't pregnant at all. She had chlamydia. I didn't know what the hell that was, but the doctor explained to Amaryllis that chlamydia is a common sexually transmitted disease (STD) that, if left untreated, can lead to ovary damage. We were both really surprised. When she told me her symptoms I never thought it could be an STD.

The doctor gave Amaryllis some pills to treat the infection. You would think that having an STD would have made her think twice before having unprotected sex the next time. But Amaryllis was so ignorant that she continued down the same path she was on before she found out she had chlamydia. This really bothered me because it never seemed to have occurred to her that as easily as she had caught chlamydia, she could catch AIDS.

I had told two other friends the same story as Amaryllis. My plan had been to tell them I wasn't a virgin, and if our friendship went back to being like it was before high school, then I would tell them the truth. They'd realize that they never had any reason to feel uncomfortable talking to me in the first place.

I told myself that I would wait about two weeks to tell them the truth. But when two weeks had passed, I told myself that I would tell them in a month. When a month passed, I told myself I would tell them on April Fool's Day. That way it would be a sort of joke I had played on them. But April Fool's Day came and went, and I still hadn't told them that I was really still a virgin.

Since they started believing that I was sexually active, they told me everything that was going on in their lives. And since I was "one of them," I had the right to help them the way I had Amaryllis because I "understood" what was going on. Back when I was a "virgin," I hadn't earned the right to advise or help them because, as far as they were concerned, I didn't have a clue as to what goes along with being sexually active. To them, I was an outsider.

There were many reasons why I kept the lie up. Most important was that I felt I was able to slow their pace, to help them realize that they shouldn't have sex with every guy they met, especially not on the first date. Once Amaryllis went out with a guy named Alex, and on their first date he took her to his apartment and they had sex. She called me after the date crying because she hadn't really wanted to do that, but he was very persistent.

Without me saying a word, she told me she was never going to put herself in that predicament again. "The next time I go out with a guy, we go to the movies or something," she told me sobbing, "and then he takes me straight home."

She said that her period hadn't come in over two months and she was feeling sick.

Amaryllis didn't change her ways immediately. It took several similar situations before she began to accept what I had been telling her all along.

It's been three years now since I first lied about being sexually active, and our friendship has grown stronger. We are like sisters who talk about everything and anything. We hang out every day and are always there for each other. If I hadn't made up that story, I don't feel they ever would have confided in me.

I've always wished I could tell them the truth, but I never do. It's not that I'm ashamed of being a virgin, it's just that my best friends feel comfortable with me now and I'm helping them in the process. Most of us confide in people who are similar to us. That way, we don't have to worry about being judged or criticized. When an alcoholic begins to realize she has a problem, for example, and is ready to get help, she goes to an Alcoholics Anonymous meeting where she can be among people who have experienced the same things.

As close as we are, however, I still can't say things are the same between my friends Susan and Amaryllis and me. I guess the way I feel now is similar to the way they used to feel towards me. Initially, they felt they had to pretend that they were still virgins like me. Once I lied, the pretending was over and they felt comfortable with me again. Now I'm the one who feels uncomfortable.

Maybe that's part of the reason I have a new best friend, Lisa. Lisa is the only close friend I have who knows I'm a virgin. She's also a virgin, which makes it really easy for me to talk to her about relationships and stuff.

For Amaryllis and Susan all relationships have to involve sex, but when I hang out with Lisa I don't have to pretend to be something I'm not. Lisa is a real best friend because she knows the real me. There's no pretending in our friendship. I confide in her more than I can confide in Amaryllis or Susan.

I know that if Amaryllis and Susan really are my best friends, they should be able to accept me for who I am. I hope that, eventually, I'll tell them the truth.

The writer was in high school when she wrote this story.

Lee Samuel

Doing the Opposite

By Donald Moore

One day last summer, my friends and I were discussing video games in an online chat room. One of my friends mentioned how he was going to buy the Sony Playstation 3 when it came out in November. "But man, the new Nintendo is gonna be wack," he said.

He knows I own almost every Nintendo product ever made, so I couldn't keep silent. "Gamecube had some great games," I replied.

"Yeah, but it's for kids," he said.

I didn't own anything Sony or play Sony games. So I could either be left out of the conversation, or I could argue about something I knew nothing about. "Playstation sucks," I said, after five minutes of deliberation.

For most people, peer pressure is when people who you consider your equals lead you to do things you wouldn't have done on your own. But what if it were reversed? What if you did the opposite of whatever your friends did? It may sound odd, but that's what my friends and I do.

Most of the time it involves trivial stuff, like me refusing to like Playstation. Or when my friends tell me to buy something, download a song or watch a show that's coming on, I argue why it's a dumb idea.

My friends act the same way. When I discuss tennis matches with my two friends who are fellow tennis fans, the rest of my friends bash the game. Rather than watch a match to see what they've been missing, they say things like "Tennis is for girls" and "Only old rich people watch tennis."

We all end up missing out on a lot of stuff because we refuse to give in to each other or 'go with the flow.'

The result? We all end up missing out on a lot of stuff because we refuse to give in to each other or "go with the flow."

Of course, sometimes resisting the influence of your friends is a good thing—there's a reason why peer pressure has such a bad reputation. Not emulating my friends has kept me out of some bad situations.

A few years ago I went to a party and everyone but me ended up getting drunk. Toward the end of the night, it was me, the lone sober kid, with a bunch of intoxicated friends. Every couple of minutes, I got the same question, with the same offended tone in their voices: "Why don't you want any?"

There were tons of reasons I could've given. But the most prominent one in my mind was that I didn't want to drink because they were doing it. The idea that I'd be drinking after they'd started made me feel like the decision wasn't mine to make. Even if I'd already been planning to drink, I'd feel like a follower.

While some teens are inclined to follow what their equals are doing, for me, my equals are just that—equal. If I did what they wanted, I'd see that as submitting. And that would mean that I'm not their equal. I've never asked my friends, but I'm pretty sure they feel the same way. None of us wants to be "led" by our friends.

I've found that independence isn't a light switch that can easily be turned on and off. The same people who listen to a great song because their friends told them to might also end up smoking just to fit in. By the same token, I don't give in to peer pressure when it's harmful, but I also end up disagreeing with friends about anything and everything, because I have a stubborn need to be independent.

Hopefully one day I'll reach some sort of balance—listening to my peers when it's to my benefit, and politely disagreeing when they have a dumb idea. Maybe I'll even try to change their minds—after all, that's what friends are for.

Donald was 18 when he wrote this story.
He is now in college, studying writing and literature.

Maurice Anderson

Trying Femininity on for Size

By Debbie Seraphin

Growing up, I was always around boys. I have two older brothers and we have always been very close. So what they did, I did. What they wore, I wore.

I climbed gates and walls, rode bikes, and played every type of sport. I dressed in baggy jeans, T-shirts, and sneakers. I had no idea what feminine was.

The fellas thought it was cool having me around, so I just enjoyed myself, not realizing how all of this was going to affect me later on in my life.

*I*n elementary school, I thought being a tomboy was cool. I didn't stand out that much because everybody dressed like a tomboy back then. The baggy style and hat-to-the-back look were in. The way of dress was very similar for both girls and boys.

When I was around 9, I noticed that other girls weren't like me. They were playing with dolls and having tea parties, things I was not allowed to do. My parents said that playing those games was like preparing to have a baby and a husband, and that I was too young to have those ideas in my head.

Since I knew my parents wouldn't allow it, I never let myself get too interested in dolls or dress up or other girls' games. I just wanted to know why other girls liked them so much.

Sometimes I would sneak dolls that my friends donated to me into the house. But when my parents found the dolls, they would immediately discard them.

To be honest, I wasn't much interested in sports either. What I did enjoy was reading, dancing, and singing. I could do those things by myself and still have a good time. But since my brothers were always playing sports and my parents made me go everywhere with them, I had no choice.

Still, I was basically happy with who I was until I arrived in junior high school. That was a period of hell. The kids would call me a tomboy because I wore baggy jeans, sweatshirts, and braids in my hair.

I dressed in baggy jeans, T-shirts, and sneakers. I had no idea what feminine was.

To make things worse, I was taller and skinnier than all the rest of the girls and I was underdeveloped. The other kids would hit me in my chest and say that they couldn't be hurting me, because I had nothing there. They would say, "Hurry up and grow. Then we won't have to hit you anymore."

One time in art class, a boy came up to me and started dissing on me for the entire period. He said, "Why do you look like you have no chest and no body? All you do is wear those dodo braids in your hair. You are so skinny and ugly. You are never going to change because you are naturally a chickenhead." I cried for the entire period while the rest of the class laughed at me. I was so embarrassed.

I believed everything everyone told me to hurt my feelings. I thought I didn't deserve to live. I went home crying every day because I did not like myself. I felt like an ugly duckling. In addition to my flat chest, I had skinny legs and knobby knees. I was always asking myself, "Why do I have to look like this, and when am I going to change?"

All of my close friends were already dating. They were pretty and smart and had everything going for them. When they were with their boyfriends, I felt left out. I never told them how I felt because I thought if I opened up, they would just mock me.

When prom night came in the 8th grade, I was determined to prove that I could fit in. This was going to be my big breakthrough. My mom and I went shopping for a new dress and shoes.

I wore an elegant purple gown with rhinestones at the straps and black slingback high-heeled pumps. My hair was done in drop curls with a bang in the front. This was the first time I had ever tried to be feminine, my big transformation.

When I first walked in, I was nervous because I didn't know how everyone was going to react to me. But I felt good in my dress and enjoyed the attention I was getting.

My friends were surprised at how nice I looked and heads actually turned. Everyone was wondering who the new girl was. I was having a good time.

Then, just when I was thinking, "I did it," something had to go wrong.

I was going into the girls' bathroom and a guy walked passed and said, "Shouldn't you be going to the boys' bathroom with me? Because you surely look like a boy to me, Shorty."

Boy, was I pissed! I wanted to curse him out but I didn't have the courage. I went home and cried instead.

I had thought this was going to be my night. After all, this was my prom night. But, no! I had to get hurt and be brought down from my one good day in that school.

I decided that when I got to high school, I was going to change. Not just in terms of the way I looked, like I did for the prom, but in terms of how I acted. I wanted to stop being so shy and easily intimidated.

When I went to school on the first day of my freshman year, I decided to study the other girls to get ideas for the new me.

I watched the way they talked, dressed, and acted. I saw the older girls always making sure that they were heard, being very sassy with teachers, and flirting with the guys in a friendly way. And they were all popular.

I thought there was only one way to be feminine and this

All of my close friends were already dating. When they were with their boyfriends, I felt left out.

was it. I didn't know anything else. So I just picked up on what I saw and copied it, even though it wasn't me. I said to myself, "If I act as they do, I might get the same reaction.

It worked. I became loud, talkative, and rude. I developed a sassy attitude and everyone seemed to like it.

I decided to change my appearance too. I processed my hair and started doing various styles that everyone enjoyed looking at. And, day by day, I would add something different to my wardrobe.

I started wearing nice small blouses instead of T-shirts, fitted jeans instead of baggy ones, and shoes instead of sneakers. People started to notice that my style was changing for the better.

My transformation was going so well that I went a little overboard. My parents had always been very strict with me, especially in terms of how I dressed. No revealing clothing was to be worn by me. But at this point in my life, I wanted attention and all eyes on me.

During my junior and senior years, I decided to rebel against my parents. I went from the nice small blouses to short belly tops, from fitted jeans to tight jeans or short skirts, and from shoes to high-heeled boots. My parents went crazy, of course, but dressing like this made me feel positive about myself.

I rebelled in other ways too. My parents were so busy trying to protect me from bad influences that they had never let me sleep out, or go hang out with my friends, or even go to the movies. I was such a "goodie two shoes" all my life—now it was time for me to spread my wings. I started to stay out late, travel around the city, and go over to my friends' houses.

My parents yelled at me, talked to my teachers, called my friends, invaded my privacy, and spied on me. It didn't work, because I was still sneaky in my own small ways. Then they gave up, deciding that I had to learn my own lesson.

At first I was having such a good time that I didn't pay my parents any mind. Then, during my senior year, I saw the pain I was putting them through and stopped all the running around.

I decided to balance my wild side with my old calmer side. Now I go out once in a while, but mostly I am busy getting through my first year of college, being an active member of my church, job-hunting, and writing in my spare time.

It's taken a long time, but I am finally happy with myself and my self-esteem is over the roof. I no longer worry about fitting in and being liked. I talk to all types of people and go to all types of places and feel accepted and respected. I love to wake up every morning and look at myself in the mirror, because I feel beautiful inside and out. I'm finally being myself and being feminine at the same time.

I never got to be myself until now. My identity always came from everybody else. When I was younger, I was a tomboy because that's what my family wanted me to be.

In junior high, I wanted to be seen as feminine, like the other girls, but I didn't know how to change. In high school, I thought there was only one way to be feminine—the rude, sarcastic, flirtatious style the other girls had. I copied their style and I finally fit in, but it still wasn't me.

Now I realize that there are many different ways of acting

feminine. There's the classy, sassy, sarcastic way, and there's the polite, respectful, calm-hearted way. Another way is a mixture of both. That's my way.

Who I am now makes everything I had to go through worth it.

So I thank all those fellas who put me through all that persecution in junior high. All of you have made me a better person.

To anyone who is now going through what I went through back then, I say: "It's going to be OK. You will survive."

Debbie was 18 when she wrote this story. She attended Bronx Community College. She also studied cosmetology.

Rudá Tillett

Thinking for Myself

By Anonymous

One day, on one of those ridiculous shopping trips that many girls find themselves embarking on for the first time around age 13, I had an interesting encounter with an image-obsessed girl.

I was walking along Canal St. in New York City with two acquaintances when it started to drizzle. Suddenly, one of the girls, Sarah, dove under a scaffolding. Seeing the confused look on my face, the other girl, Rachel, giggled and said, "She doesn't want to get her hair wet."

I found out afterwards that Sarah cared so much about her hair because she'd spent hours flat-ironing it and didn't want the rain to "ruin" it.

I was confused about why it was such a big deal. I asked Rachel why it mattered so much what her hair looked like. She just shrugged off the question. I assumed that spending so much energy to look pretty must be normal, and of course I wanted to be normal.

So, despite the fact that I already had stick-straight brown hair, I simply couldn't wait for the chance to flat-iron it. I thought to myself, "This is what it's going to take to make me attractive." Pretty soon I found myself in a constant haze of worry that I wasn't good enough.

*P*ressure from my friends wasn't the only reason I gave into mainstream culture's idea of what I should look like. As Jehovah's Witnesses, my parents had always warned me to resist the pressure of commercialism. During countless Jehovah's Witness meetings, the speaker would encourage everyone to reject modern fashion and dress conservatively.

But there were women at those meetings wearing pointy-toed shoes that cost hundreds of dollars. One man in the congregation even had a job doing interior design for Armani. Granted, this didn't account for all Jehovah's Witnesses, but in a religion that calls for modesty, these individuals seemed strangely placed. I was confused from a very early age by the mixed messages my religion seemed to be sending me.

So when I turned 13 and hit that typical rebellion phase, I figured the best way to rebel was to buy into mainstream consumer culture. I wanted to adhere to everything my religion wasn't, and I worked to become as much like the rest of the world as possible. I was a marketer's dream.

At the same time, all my waking hours were spent in school and sitting at church listening to very strategically planned brainwashing discussions about how it was our duty to uphold some sort of Christian fantasy of what our appearance should be. My parents even started locking me in our apartment to keep me away from outside influences.

Feeling constant pressure from two opposing worlds, I began functioning on autopilot and eventually did very little thinking for myself. At times I felt absolutely numb, and I don't doubt that for months at a time I was a complete zombie.

It was difficult to know anything about who I was or what I wanted, when there was such a steady flow of information from my parents telling me to button up my shirt and magazine ads telling me to unbutton it. As a result I had a very messy identity.

By the time I was 16, I was sick of it. No matter where I went outside my home, I felt constant pressure to be the conventionally pretty, innocent blonde or the typically skinny, edgy brunette with a cigarette.

I was confused from a very early age by the mixed messages my religion seemed to be sending me.

I was neurotic and unhappy about who I was becoming—a person who grew more shallow each day. I worried that if I didn't get out of New York, I'd lose the strength to resist the pressure from my parents, friends and advertising.

A friend of mine from Denver, Colorado had been visiting New York that summer. Now that fall was approaching, she was going home and we met to say our goodbyes over bad pizza.

"It's a bummer you're leaving," I told her. "I can't stand it in New York, and now you won't even be here!" The thought of her leaving forced me to admit how unhappy I was with my friends and family, and with the person I'd become.

"You should come to Denver!" she said.

"There's no way I'd be able to," I laughed. "What an absurd idea."

"No! Really! You can stay with me!"

I thought about it a minute and wondered how my leaving would affect my family. Then I realized that I'd spent years going along with ideas that were not my own.

If my mom and dad could find it in themselves to lock me inside our apartment in the name of God, I could stand to leave the state in the name of a chance.

I needed a cleansing period free from the pressures of religion and media. I had to reestablish my values, and my associates from birth to age 15 were not the people to be doing it with. I felt that they wouldn't care for me in the same way if I strayed from my flat-ironed hair and tight, ill-fitting Abercrombie clothing.

"OK," I finally said. "I'm gonna do it."

I told a close friend of mine about my situation and asked if he could buy me a ticket. Within half an hour he booked a one-way flight for me, and a week later I took a plane to Denver.

I felt amazing. I could finally get out for the first time in my life. I know not many people get the opportunity to ditch everything that makes them unhappy as easily as I did, but I was fortunate enough to have the chance to do it, so I took it. I ended up telling only a handful of people (I didn't tell my parents). I had no remorse for leaving my family and "friends" whose whole lives, I believed, were founded on being fake.

During my year in Denver as a runaway, my life was almost completely void of media. I didn't have a cell phone, TV, or radio. I didn't go to any malls or use the Internet. Slowly, I became a different person.

But it wasn't all these things that caused the change. The biggest influence was the people I met. Unlike my old friends in New York, my new friends were unmoved by ad culture. They made their own clothes and refused to support any big chain stores. They truly thought for themselves, instead of letting advertisements or religion dictate how they should be or dress.

I lived in a progressive community, where people cared about gender issues and took community work seriously. I lived in a house with five other people in their early 20s. They were boys and girls who were bent on fighting the clean-cut capitalists we all hated for their ignorance and power.

My friends were punks. They were tattooed and pierced to all degrees. They had warm hearts and even warmer values, which they showed in their daily efforts to improve society. They worked for Food Not Bombs, providing free meals to the hungry, ran volunteer book collectives with activist, feminist and anarchist literature, and also ran volunteer bike collectives, teaching anyone in the community about building bikes for free.

Eventually I got a job working at an art gallery and café, but until then, I had every one of my Denver friends to thank for always making sure that I was taken care of. Two of my friends even made me a bike. They came to my job one day and brought it along with them. That gesture was unlike anything anyone had ever done for me before.

My parents were telling me to button up my shirt and magazine ads were telling me to unbutton it.

At that moment I realized people need to take care of each other, no matter what. I wanted to be able to alter people's lives like they had just altered mine. I never would've felt strongly about this had I not visited Denver. Instead I'd probably still be unaware of what I wanted, and would probably care very little about helping anyone else.

One of my fondest Denver memories is when I went to a demonstration against sweatshops. The main speaker used to work in sweatshops and now leads rallies against Gap, Old Navy, Banana Republic, Abercrombie and Fitch, and other companies that use sweatshop labor.

She talked about the long hours and low pay, about pregnant women being fired because they couldn't complete their tasks on time. Hearing about what life is like working in a sweatshop was one of the most intense learning experiences of my life.

As I listened to her, I looked down and began to analyze everything I was wearing. I imagined someone working 40 hours straight, trying to meet a deadline of a hundred jeans per hour, and almost fainting from the heat of an overcrowded warehouse.

After this experience it became simple for me to start rejecting commercialism. I became more aware of how advertisements and commercials are the economy's lifeblood—the average American views 3,000 ads a day, according to Jean Kilbourne's

Deadly Persuasion, a book about how advertising influences and manipulates women and girls.

Without ads, how would people know just what kind of bed sheets to use? What kind of fabric softener to throw in to make the bed sheets soft? What type of clothes to wear, how worn and full of holes their $100 dollar jeans should be? What car to drive, liquor to drink, cigarettes to smoke to attract the right kind of man or woman into those bed sheets? Without them, people would have to do just what I was learning to do in Denver—they would have to think for themselves.

I'd been taught that I needed to please everybody else. Now I saw that I needed to change the way I thought before I did any more damage to my self-esteem. I began to want to resist advertising not for the sake of "modesty," as my parents had taught me, but because of everything it represented—sweatshop labor, greed, and the manipulation of young minds.

E ventually, I decided to come back to New York because I wanted to finish high school. My parents, frightened by my running away, welcomed me back home with relief. But I was still worried about what awaited me there. In addition to my anxiety and sadness about leaving my friends in Denver, I feared that I wouldn't find any form of community once I arrived back in New York. I already suspected I'd have to cut all ties with my old New York friends.

My fears weren't unfounded. Even before I got back, word about me not shaving my legs spread like a wildfire among people I used to know. Needless to say, they didn't approve.

And when I did come back, the first thing one of my old friends asked me was whether I'd seen how much weight a formerly chubby girlfriend of ours had lost. I just felt disgusted and said nothing. I haven't seen any of these people since. Instead, I've been working to find a group of friends who share my values.

Getting used to the constant onslaught of ads and commercialism I ran away from hasn't been easy either. I remember my first subway ride when I came back from Denver in August, my first subway ride in a year. The train howled and screeched into the station and the doors opened with that obnoxious "ding-dong," like mechanical harps welcoming me into a heaven of ads.

People parted to make a small space on the cluttered train for me. To my left, right, and even above my head on both walls of the train, there were advertisements for everything from vodka and storage space to Coach bags, Coca-Cola, and iPods. I noticed how white iPod headphone cords drooped from almost every other passenger's head, and Coach bags hung from their arms.

My anxiety mounted, and all I could say to myself was, "Here we go again." I'd have to learn how to cope with it, since I'd have to endure this form of transportation for as long as I lived in New York. Especially since my handmade bike had been stolen soon after I moved back.

It's become easier to find happiness now that I have my own set of values by which I live my life. My parents recognize this and have ceased pressuring me into rigid forms of religious worship. I've begun to openly criticize their methods and beliefs, and I think this had led them to back off.

One day, a few weeks after I returned, my mom asked me why I didn't shave my legs. So instead of telling her why I didn't, I decided to ask her why she did. Her reply was, "I think it's feminine to shave your legs." This response astounded me. She went on to say that women who don't shave their legs are usually lesbians. When I asked her if she would treat me differently if I were a lesbian, she said she didn't know.

But this time I didn't feel the need to run away from her pressure or anyone else's. I simply walked away. Thanks to Denver, I can gladly say that I am completely comfortable with who I am. Now I don't have to get on a plane to feel grounded.

The writer was in high school when she wrote this story.

James Faber

Hear No Evil, See No Evil... Do No Evil

By Curtis Holmes

When I was younger, I was pretty upset that my parents gave me so many responsibilities and had so many rules, and that I had to come home right after school every day and watch my little sister.

But when I watched my friend get in big trouble, it made me think that maybe my responsibilities were a blessing in disguise, and in some ways it made me be even more strict with myself than my parents were with me.

I mean, if my godbrother could go to church for years and still get lured into street life, couldn't that happen to me? I am not making any excuses for him—he was lured, not pushed. But if you had asked me before, I would never have expected my friend to get in trouble like this.

So who is to say what could happen? There are hundreds of stories about people with so much promise who have failed, which is why I put pressure on myself to succeed and not mess up.

The way I live my life every day is far different from how other people live theirs. I come home, take care of my homework, study, read, and watch my sister. I look at TV and sometimes I go outside. But I don't hang out too much with the kids in my neighborhood, or go to parties or stay out late.

I put pressure on myself to succeed and not mess up.

You'll never see me drinking or smoking. Besides school and sleep, church takes up most of the rest of my week. There are services on Tuesday, Thursday, and Sunday. And every month there are youth meetings at church, where I have most of my friends.

And one thing I never do is treat a challenge as unimportant, no matter what it is.

Horses at a racetrack wear blinders on the sides of their eyes. That's so that they can't look to the right or left and get distracted while they're racing.

I'm like those horses. I don't look to my left and see the drugs and alcohol. I will not look to my right and see the sex. I will only look ahead to finish the race.

Sometimes the blinders prevent me from doing things that regular teens do. Sometimes I feel I'm stuck with my little sister after school, cooking and cleaning like a maid. Sometimes I want to party all night, do all the things I just said I will never do. I want to be the big willie who has everybody wanting to be like him.

Though I have some good friends who I've had for a while, I don't make that many new friends and I don't have a girlfriend. You can ask my friend Michelle. She'll tell you that most of the time when I'm alone and looking sad, it's not because something is wrong. It's just that I'm not used to being with people a lot, which makes me anti-social.

I know that by living this lifestyle I might miss out on a lot of things and a lot of interesting people, but that's something that I can live with. I just tell myself that anything I can do now with a girl for a month or two, I will be able to do with my wife forever. I can blast my stereo and dance until the sun comes up in my house, instead of going to a party.

Also, I can stand over a factory pipe, inhale the smoke into my lungs, and feel like a smoker. Or better yet, I can save myself the effort of getting involved in gang violence and just jump out a window right now. You get what I am saying?

I know most teens would look at my life and say I'm crazy. They might think that any teen would live a life like mine only because he has parents who like to torture him.

But I don't mind my parents' rules, and I've made some of the rules myself. Because when I think of my friend, I think that I could have been the one who got caught up in street life. So I'm planning to stay as far away from trouble as I can.

Curtis was 14 when he wrote this story.

Townsend Press

Lost and Found

Darcy Wills winced at the loud rap music coming from her sister's room.

> My rhymes were rockin'
> MC's were droppin'
> People shoutin' and hip-hoppin'
> Step to me and you'll be inferior
> 'Cause I'm your lyrical superior.

Darcy went to Grandma's room. The darkened room smelled of lilac perfume, Grandma's favorite, but since her stroke Grandma did not notice it, or much of anything.

"Bye, Grandma," Darcy whispered from the doorway. "I'm going to school now."

Just then, the music from Jamee's room cut off, and Jamee rushed into the hallway.

The teen characters in the Bluford novels, a fiction series by Townsend Press, struggle with many of the same difficult issues as the writers in this book. Here's the first chapter from *Lost and Found*, by Anne Scraff, the first book in the series. In this novel, high school sophomore Darcy contends with the return of her long-absent father, the troubling behavior of her younger sister Jamee, and the beginning of her first relationship.

"Like she even hears you," Jamee said as she passed Darcy. Just two years younger than Darcy, Jamee was in eighth grade, though she looked older.

"It's still nice to talk to her. Sometimes she understands. You want to pretend she's not here or something?"

"She's not," Jamee said, grabbing her backpack.

"Did you study for your math test?" Darcy asked. Mom was an emergency room nurse who worked rotating shifts. Most of the time, Mom was too tired to pay much attention to the girls' schoolwork. So Darcy tried to keep track of Jamee.

"Mind your own business," Jamee snapped.

"You got two D's on your last report card," Darcy scolded. "You wanna flunk?" Darcy did not want to sound like a nagging parent, but Jamee wasn't doing her best. Maybe she couldn't make A's like Darcy, but she could do better.

Jamee stomped out of the apartment, slamming the door behind her. "Mom's trying to get some rest!" Darcy yelled. "Do you have to be so selfish?" But Jamee was already gone, and the apartment was suddenly quiet.

Darcy loved her sister. Once, they had been good friends. But now all Jamee cared about was her new group of rowdy friends. They leaned on cars outside of school and turned up rap music on their boom boxes until the street seemed to tremble like an earthquake. Jamee had even stopped hanging out with her old friend Alisha Wrobel, something she used to do every weekend.

Darcy went back into the living room, where her mother sat in the recliner sipping coffee. "I'll be home at 2:30, Mom," Darcy said. Mom smiled faintly. She was tired, always tired. And lately she was worried too. The hospital where she worked was cutting staff. It seemed each day fewer people were expected to do more work. It was like trying to climb a mountain that keeps getting taller as you go. Mom was forty-four, but just yesterday she said, "I'm like an old car that's run out of warranty, baby. You know what happens then. Old car is ready for the junk heap. Well, maybe that hospital is gonna tell me one of these days—'Mattie Mae Wills, we don't need you anymore. We can get somebody younger and cheaper.'"

"Mom, you're not old at all," Darcy had said, but they were only words, empty words. They could not erase the dark, weary lines from beneath her mother's eyes.

Darcy headed down the street toward Bluford High School. It was not a terrible neighborhood they lived in; it just was not good. Many front yards were not cared for. Debris—fast food wrappers, plastic bags, old newspapers—blew around and piled against fences and curbs. Darcy hated that. Sometimes she and other kids from school spent Saturday mornings cleaning up, but it seemed a losing battle. Now, as she walked, she tried to focus on small spots of beauty along the way. Mrs. Walker's pink and white roses bobbed proudly in the morning breeze. The Hustons' rock garden was carefully designed around a wooden windmill.

As she neared Bluford, Darcy thought about the science project that her biology teacher, Ms. Reed, was assigning. Darcy was doing hers on tidal pools. She was looking forward to visiting a real tidal pool, taking pictures, and doing research. Today, Ms. Reed would be dividing the students into teams of two. Darcy wanted to be paired with her close friend, Brisana Meeks. They were both excellent students, a cut above most kids at Bluford, Darcy thought.

"Today, we are forming project teams so that each student can gain something valuable from the other," Ms. Reed said as Darcy sat at her desk. Ms. Reed was a tall, stately woman who reminded Darcy of the Statue of Liberty. She would have been a perfect model for the statue if Lady Liberty had been a black woman. She never would have been called pretty, but it was possible she might have been called a handsome woman. "For this assignment, each of you will be working with someone you've never worked with before."

Darcy was worried. If she was not teamed with Brisana,

maybe she would be teamed with some really dumb student who would pull her down. Darcy was a little ashamed of herself for thinking that way. Grandma used to say that all flowers are equal, but different. The simple daisy was just as lovely as the prize rose. But still Darcy did not want to be paired with some weak partner who would lower her grade.

"Darcy Wills will be teamed with Tarah Carson," Ms. Reed announced.

Darcy gasped. Not Tarah! Not that big, chunky girl with the brassy voice who squeezed herself into tight skirts and wore lime green or hot pink satin tops and cheap jewelry. Not Tarah who hung out with Cooper Hodden, that loser who was barely hanging on to his football eligibility. Darcy had heard that Cooper had been left back once or twice and even got his driver's license as a sophomore. Darcy's face felt hot with anger. Why was Ms. Reed doing this?

Hakeem Randall, a handsome, shy boy who sat in the back row, was teamed with the class blabbermouth, LaShawn Appleby. Darcy had a secret crush on Hakeem since freshman year. So far she had only shared this with her diary, never with another living soul.

It was almost as though Ms. Reed was playing some devilish game. Darcy glanced at Tarah, who was smiling broadly. Tarah had an enormous smile, and her teeth contrasted harshly with her dark red lipstick. "Great," Darcy muttered under her breath.

Ms. Reed ord e red the teams to meet so they could begin to plan their projects.

As she sat down by Tarah, Darcy was instantly sickened by a syrupy-sweet odor.

She must have doused herself with cheap perfume this morning , Darcy thought.

"Hey, girl," Tarah said. "Well, don't you look down in the mouth. What's got you lookin' that way?"

It was hard for Darcy to meet new people, especially someone like Tarah, a person Aunt Charlotte would call "low class." These were people who were loud and rude. They drank too much, used drugs, got into fights and ruined the neighborhood. They yelled ugly insults at people, even at their friends. Darcy did not actually know that Tarah did anything like this personally, but she seemed like the type who did.

"I just didn't think you'd be interested in tidal pools," Darcy explained.

Tarah slammed her big hand on the desk, making her gold bracelets jangle like ice cubes in a glass, and laughed. Darcy had never heard a mule bray, but she was sure it made exactly the same sound. Then Tarah leaned close and whispered, "Girl, I don't know a tidal pool from a fool. Ms. Reed stuck us together to mess with our heads, you hear what I'm sayin'?"

"Maybe we could switch to other partners," Darcy said nervously.

A big smile spread slowly over Tarah's face. "Nah, I think I'm gonna enjoy this. You're always sittin' here like a princess collecting your A's. Now you gotta work with a regular person, so you better loosen up, girl!"

Darcy felt as if her teeth were glued to her tongue. She fumbled in her bag for her outline of the project. It all seemed like a horrible joke now. She and Tarah Carson standing knee-deep in the muck of a tidal pool!

"Worms live there, don't they?" Tarah asked, twisting a big gold ring on her chubby finger.

"Yeah, I guess," Darcy replied.

"Big green worms," Tarah continued. "So if you get your feet stuck in the bottom of that old tidal pool, and you can't get out, do the worms crawl up your clothes?"

Darcy ignored the remark. "I'd like for us to go there soon, you know, look around."

"My boyfriend, Cooper, he goes down to the ocean all the time. He can take us. He says he's seen these fiddler crabs. They look like big spiders, and they'll try to bite your toes off. Cooper says so," Tarah said.

"Stop being silly," Darcy shot back. "If you're not even going to be serious . . . "

"You think you're better than me, don't you?" Tarah suddenly growled.

"I never said—" Darcy blurted.

"You don't have to say it, girl. It's in your eyes. You think I'm a low-life and you're something special. Well, I got more friends than you got fingers and toes together. You got no friends, and everybody laughs at you behind your back. Know what the word on you is? Darcy Wills give you the chills."

Just then, the bell rang, and Darcy was glad for the excuse to turn away from Tarah, to hide the hot tears welling in her eyes. She quickly rushed from the classroom, relieved that school was over. Darcy did not think she could bear to sit through another class just now.

Darcy headed down the long street towards home. She did not like Tarah. Maybe it was wrong, but it was true. Still, Tarah's brutal words hurt. Even stupid, awful people might tell you the truth about yourself. And Darcy did not have any real friends, except for Brisana. Maybe the other kids were mocking her behind her back. Darcy was very slender, not as shapely as many of the other girls. She remembered the time when Cooper Hodden was hanging in front of the deli with his friends, and he yelled as Darcy went by, "Hey, is that really a female there? Sure don't look like it. Looks more like an old broomstick with hair. " His companions laughed rudely, and Darcy had walked a little faster.

A terrible thought clawed at Darcy. Maybe she was the loser, not Tarah. Tarah was always hanging with a bunch of kids, laughing and joking. She would go down the hall to the lockers and greetings would come from everywhere. "Hey, Tarah!" "What's up, Tar?" "See ya at lunch, girl." When Darcy went to the lockers, there was dead silence.

Darcy usually glanced into stores on her way home from school. She enjoyed looking at the trays of chicken feet and pork ears at the little Asian grocery store. Sometimes she would even steal a glance at the diners sitting by the picture window at the Golden Grill Restaurant. But today she stared straight ahead, her shoulders drooping.

If this had happened last year, she would have gone directly to Grandma's house, a block from where Darcy lived. How many times had Darcy and Jamee run to Grandma's, eaten applesauce cookies, drunk cider, and poured out their troubles to Grandma. Somehow, their problems would always dissolve in the warmth of her love and wisdom. But now Grandma was a frail figure in the corner of their apartment, saying little. And what little she did say made less and less sense.

Darcy was usually the first one home. The minute she got there, Mom left for the hospital to take the 3:00 to 11:00 shift in the ER. By the time Mom finished her paperwork at the hospital, she would be lucky to be home again by midnight. After Mom left, Darcy went to Grandma's room to give her the malted nutrition drink that the doctor ordered her to have three times a day.

"Want to drink your chocolate malt, Grandma?" Darcy asked, pulling up a chair beside Grandma's bed.

Grandma was sitting up, and her eyes were open. "No. I'm not hungry," she said listlessly. She always said that.

"You need to drink your malt, Grandma," Darcy insisted, gently putting the straw between the pinched lips.

Grandma sucked the malt slowly. "Grandma, nobody likes me at school," Darcy said. She did not expect any response. But there was a strange comfort in telling Grandma anyway. "Everybody laughs at me. It's because I'm shy and maybe stuck-up, too, I guess. But I don't mean to be. Stuck-up, I mean. Maybe I'm weird. I could be weird, I guess. I could be like Aunt Charlotte . . ." Tears rolled down Darcy's cheeks. Her heart ached with loneliness. There was nobody to talk to anymore, nobody who had time to listen, nobody who understood.

Grandma blinked and pushed the straw away. Her eyes brightened as they did now and then. "You are a wonderful girl. Everybody knows that," Grandma said in an almost normal voice. It happened like that sometimes. It was like being in the middle of a dark storm and having the clouds part, revealing a patch of clear, sunlit blue. For just a few precious minutes, Grandma was bright-eyed and saying normal things.

"Oh, Grandma, I'm so lonely," Darcy cried, pressing her head against Grandma's small shoulder.

"You were such a beautiful baby," Grandma said, stroking her hair." 'That one is going to shine like the morning star.' That's what I told your Mama. 'That child is going to shine like the morning star.' Tell me, Angelcake, is your daddy home yet?"

Darcy straightened. "Not yet." Her heart pounded so hard, she could feel it thumping in her chest. Darcy's father had not been home in five years.

"Well, tell him to see me when he gets home. I want him to buy you that blue dress you liked in the store window. That's for you, Angelcake. Tell him I've got money. My social security came, you know. I have money for the blue dress," Grandma said, her eyes slipping shut.

Just then, Darcy heard the apartment door slam. Jamee had come home. Now she stood in the hall, her hands belligerently on her hips. "Are you talking to Grandma again?" Jamee demanded.

"She was talking like normal," Darcy said. "Sometimes she does. You know she does."

"That is so stupid," Jamee snapped. "She never says anything right anymore. Not anything!" Jamee's voice trembled.

Darcy got up quickly and set down the can of malted milk. She ran to Jamee and put her arms around her sister. "Jamee, I know you're hurting too."

"Oh, don't be stupid," Jamee protested, but Darcy hugged

her more tightly, and in a few seconds Jamee was crying. "She was the best thing in this stupid house," Jamee cried. "Why'd she have to go?"

"She didn't go," Darcy said. "Not really."

"She did! She did!" Jamee sobbed. She struggled free of Darcy, ran to her room, and slammed the door. In a minute, Darcy heard the bone-rattling sound of rap music.

Lost and Found, *a Bluford Series™ novel, is reprinted with permission from Townsend Press. Copyright © 2002.*

Want to read more? This and other *Bluford Series™* novels and paperbacks can be purchased for $1 each at www.townsendpress.com.

Teens:
How to Get More Out of This Book

Self-help: The teens who wrote the stories in this book did so because they hope that telling their stories will help readers who are facing similar challenges. They want you to know that you are not alone, and that taking specific steps can help you manage or overcome very difficult situations. They've done their best to be clear about the actions that worked for them so you can see if they'll work for you.

Writing: You can also use the book to improve your writing skills. Each teen in this book wrote 5-10 drafts of his or her story before it was published. If you read the stories closely you'll see that the teens work to include a beginning, a middle, and an end, and good scenes, description, dialogue, and anecdotes (little stories). To improve your writing, take a look at how these writers construct their stories. Try some of their techniques in your own writing.

Reading: Finally, you'll notice that we include the first chapter from a Bluford Series novel in this book, alongside the true stories by teens. We hope you'll like it enough to continue reading. The more you read, the more you'll strengthen your reading skills. Teens at Youth Communication like the Bluford novels because they explore themes similar to those in their own stories. Your school may already have the Bluford books. If not, you can order them online for only $1.

Resources on the Web

We will occasionally post Think About It questions on our website, www.youthcomm.org, to accompany stories in this and other Youth Communication books. We try out the questions with teens and post the ones they like best. Many teens report that writing answers to those questions in a journal is very helpful.

How to Use This Book in Staff Training

Staff say that reading these stories gives them greater insight into what teens are thinking and feeling, and new strategies for working with them. You can help the staff you work with by using these stories as case studies.

Select one story to read in the group, and ask staff to identify and discuss the main issue facing the teen. There may be disagreement about this, based on the background and experience of staff. That is fine. One point of the exercise is that teens have complex lives and needs. Adults can probably be more effective if they don't focus too narrowly and can see several dimensions of their clients.

Ask staff: What issues or feelings does the story provoke in them? What kind of help do they think the teen wants? What interventions are likely to be most promising? Least effective? Why? How would you build trust with the teen writer? How have other adults failed the teen, and how might that affect his or her willingness to accept help? What other resources would be helpful to this teen, such as peer support, a mentor, counseling, family therapy, etc.

Resources on the Web

From time to time we will post Think About It questions on our website, www.youthcomm.org, to accompany stories in this and other Youth Communication books. We try out the questions with teens and post the ones that they find most effective. We'll also post lesson for some of the stories. Adults can use the questions and lessons in workshops.

Discussion Guide

Teachers and Staff:
How to Use This Book in Groups

When working with teens individually or in groups, using these stories can help young people face difficult issues in a way that feels safe to them. That's because talking about the issues in the stories usually feels safer to teens than talking about those same issues in their own lives. Addressing issues through the stories allows for some personal distance; they hit close to home, but not too close. Talking about them opens up a safe place for reflection. As teens gain confidence talking about the issues in the stories, they usually become more comfortable talking about those issues in their own lives.

Below are general questions that can help you lead discussions about the stories, which help teens and staff reflect on the issues in their own work and lives. In most cases you can read a story and conduct a discussion in one 45-minute session. Teens are usually happy to read the stories aloud, with each teen reading a paragraph or two. (Allow teens to pass if they don't want to read.) It takes 10-15 minutes to read a story straight through. However, it is often more effective to let workshop participants make comments and discuss the story as you go along. The workshop leader may even want to annotate her copy of the story beforehand with key questions.

If teens read the story ahead of time or silently, it's good to break the ice with a few questions that get everyone on the same page: Who is the main character? How old is she? What happened to her? How did she respond? Etc. Another good starting question is: "What stood out for you in the story?" Go around the room and let each person briefly mention one thing.

Then move on to open-ended questions, which encourage participants to think more deeply about what the writers were feeling, the choices they faced, and they actions they took. There are no right or wrong answers to the open-ended questions. Open-ended questions encourage participants to think about how the themes, emotions and choices in the stories relate to their own lives. Here are some examples of open-ended questions that we have found to be effective. You can use variations of these questions with almost any story in this book.

—What main problem or challenge did the writer face?

—What choices did the teen have in trying to deal with the problem?

—Which way of dealing with the problem was most effective for the teen? Why?

—What strengths, skills, or resources did the teen use to address the challenge?

—If you were in the writer's shoes, what would you have done?

—What could adults have done better to help this young person?

—What have you learned by reading this story that you didn't know before?

—What, if anything, will you do differently after reading this story?

—What surprised you in this story?

—Do you have a different view of this issue, or see a different way of dealing with it, after reading this story? Why or why not?

Credits

The stories in this book originally appeared in the following Youth Communication publications:

"My Secret Love," by Anonymous, *Represent*, September/October 2000

"Losing My Friends to Weed," by Jamel Salter, *Represent*, January/February 1994

"Why Do So Many Teens Cheat?" by Fan Yi Mok, *New Youth Connections*, May/June 2001

"Can't Afford to Follow," by Charlene George, *New Youth Connections*, March 2007

"Hiding My Talent No More," by Jesselin Rodriguez, *New Youth Connections*, December 1996

"Why I Speak My Mind," by Desiree Bailey, *New Youth Connections*, March 2007

"Sex Doesn't Make You a Man," by Damon Washington, *New Youth Connections*, September/October 1996

"My So-Called Friends," by Sharon Feder, *New Youth Connections*, September/October 2001

"Making Me Dance," by Jill Feigelman, *New Youth Connections*, March 2007

"Peer Pressure Ended Our Relationship," by Lenny Jones, *Represent*, July/August 1997

"My Bad," by V.P., *Represent*, September/October 2000

"The Pastor's Daughter," by Natalia Tavarez, *New Youth Connections*, December 2007

"I Wanted to Be Pretty and Popular," by Sabrina Rencher, *New Youth Connections*, April 2001

"The Trouble With Being a Virgin," by Anonymous, *New Youth Connections*, November 1996

"Doing the Opposite," by Donald Moore, *New Youth Connections*, March 2007

"Trying Femininity on for Size," by Debbie Seraphin, *New Youth Connections*, March 1999

"Thinking for Myself," by Anonymous, *New Youth Connections*, March 2006

"Hear No Evil, See No Evil... Do No Evil?" *New Youth Connections*, September 1998

About
Youth Communication

Youth Communication, founded in 1980, is a nonprofit youth development program located in New York City whose mission is to teach writing, journalism, and leadership skills. The teenagers we train become writers for our websites and books and for two print magazines, *New Youth Connections*, a general-interest youth magazine, and *Represent*, a magazine by and for young people in foster care.

Each year, up to 100 young people participate in Youth Communication's school-year and summer journalism workshops where they work under the direction of full-time professional editors. Most are African American, Latino, or Asian, and many are recent immigrants. The opportunity to reach their peers with accurate portrayals of their lives and important self-help information motivates the young writers to create powerful stories.

Our goal is to run a strong youth development program in which teens produce high quality stories that inform and inspire their peers. Doing so requires us to be sensitive to the complicated lives and emotions of the teen participants while also providing an intellectually rigorous experience. We achieve that goal in the writing/teaching/editing relationship, which is the core of our program.

Our teaching and editorial process begins with discussions

between adult editors and the teen staff. In those meetings, the teens and the editors work together to identify the most important issues in the teens' lives and to figure out how those issues can be turned into stories that will resonate with teen readers.

Once story topics are chosen, students begin the process of crafting their stories. For a personal story, that means revisiting events in one's past to understand their significance for the future. For a commentary, it means developing a logical and persuasive point of view. For a reported story, it means gathering information through research and interviews. Students look inward and outward as they try to make sense of their experiences and the world around them and find the points of intersection between personal and social concerns. That process can take a few weeks or a few months. Stories frequently go through ten or more drafts as students work under the guidance of their editors, the way any professional writer does.

Many of the students who walk through our doors have uneven skills, as a result of poor education, living under extremely stressful conditions, or coming from homes where English is a second language. Yet, to complete their stories, students must successfully perform a wide range of activities, including writing and rewriting, reading, discussion, reflection, research, interviewing, and typing. They must work as members of a team and they must accept individual responsibility. They learn to provide constructive criticism, and to accept it. They engage in explorations of truthfulness, fairness, and accuracy. They meet deadlines. They must develop the audacity to believe that they have something important to say and the humility to recognize that saying it well is not a process of instant gratification. Rather, it usually requires a long, hard struggle through many discussions and much rewriting.

It would be impossible to teach these skills and dispositions as separate, disconnected topics, like grammar, ethics, or assertiveness. However, we find that students make rapid progress when they are learning skills in the context of an inquiry that is personally significant to them and that will benefit their peers.

When teens publish their stories—in *New Youth Connections* and *Represent*, on the web, and in other publications—they reach tens of thousands of teen and adult readers. Teachers, counselors, social workers, and other adults circulate the stories to young people in their classes and out-of-school youth programs. Adults tell us that teens in their programs—including many who are ordinarily resistant to reading—clamor for the stories. Teen readers report that the stories give them information they can't get anywhere else, and inspire them to reflect on their lives and open lines of communication with adults.

Writers usually participate in our program for one semester, though some stay much longer. Years later, many of them report that working here was a turning point in their lives—that it helped them acquire the confidence and skills that they needed for success in college and careers. Scores of our graduates have overcome tremendous obstacles to become journalists, writers, and novelists. They include National Book Award finalist Edwidge Danticat, novelist Ernesto Quinonez, writer Veronica Chambers and *New York Times* reporter Rachel Swarns. Hundreds more are working in law, business, and other careers. Many are teachers, principals, and youth workers, and several have started nonprofit youth programs themselves and work as mentors— helping another generation of young people develop their skills and find their voices.

Youth Communication is a nonprofit educational corporation. Contributions are gratefully accepted and are tax deductible to the fullest extent of the law.

To make a contribution, or for information about our publications and programs, including our catalog of over 100 books and curricula for hard-to-reach teens, see www.youthcomm.org

About The Editors

Al Desetta has been an editor of Youth Communication's two teen magazines, *Foster Care Youth United* (now known as *Represent*) and *New Youth Connections*. He was also an instructor in Youth Communication's juvenile prison writing program. In 1991, he became the organization's first director of teacher development, working with high school teachers to help them produce better writers and student publications.

Prior to working at Youth Communication, Desetta directed environmental education projects in New York City public high schools and worked as a reporter.

He has a master's degree in English literature from City College of the City University of New York and a bachelor's degree from the State University of New York at Binghamton, and he was a Revson Fellow at Columbia University for the 1990-91 academic year.

He is the editor of many books, including several other Youth Communication anthologies: *The Heart Knows Something Different: Teenage Voices from the Foster Care System, The Struggle to Be Strong,* and *The Courage to Be Yourself*. He is currently a freelance editor.

Keith Hefner co-founded Youth Communication in 1980 and has directed it ever since. He is the recipient of the Luther P. Jackson Education Award from the New York Association of Black Journalists and a MacArthur Fellowship. He was also a Revson Fellow at Columbia University.

Laura Longhine is the editorial director at Youth Communication. She edited *Represent*, Youth Communication's magazine by and for youth in foster care, for three years, and has written for a variety of publications. She has a BA in English from Tufts University and an MS in Journalism from Columbia University.

More Helpful Books
From Youth Comunication

The Struggle to Be Strong: True Stories by Teens About Overcoming Tough Times. Foreword by Veronica Chambers. Help young people identify and build on their own strengths with 30 personal stories about resiliency. (Free Spirit)

Starting With "I": Personal Stories by Teenagers. "Who am I and who do I want to become?" Thirty-five stories examine this question through the lens of race, ethnicity, gender, sexuality, family, and more. Increase this book's value with the free Teacher's Guide, available from youthcomm.org. (Youth Communication)

Real Stories, Real Teens. Inspire teens to read and recognize their strengths with this collection of 26 true stories by teens. The young writers describe how they overcame significant challenges and stayed true to themselves. Also includes the first chapters from three novels in the Bluford Series. (Youth Communication)

The Courage to Be Yourself: True Stories by Teens About Cliques, Conflicts, and Overcoming Peer Pressure. In 26 first-person stories, teens write about their lives with searing honesty. These stories will inspire young readers to reflect on their own lives, work through their problems, and help them discover who they really are. (Free Spirit)

Out With It: Gay and Straight Teens Write About Homosexuality. Break stereotypes and provide support with this unflinching look at gay life from a teen's perspective. With a focus on urban youth, this book also includes several heterosexual teens' transformative experiences with gay peers. (Youth Communication)